You Are Smarter Than You Think*!*

You Are Smarter Than You Think*!*

Using Your Brain the Way It Was Designed
The Missing Piece to Success

Renée Mollan-Masters, M.A.

Third Edition

Grateful acknowledgment to the following for permission granted for reprinting copyrighted material for: Men Are From Mars and Women Are From Venus by John Gray. Copyright ©1992 by John Gray. Reprinted by permission of Harper Collins Publishers, Inc.

Published by Reality Productions
6245 Old Highway 99 South
Ashland, OR 97520

Edition one Published 1992
Edition two Published 1997
Copyright © 2009 by Renée Mollan-Masters

Mollan-Masters, Renée.
   You *are smarter than you think!* : Using Your Brain the Way It Was Designed / Renée Mollan-Masters. —3rd ed.

Includes index.
ISBN 978-0-984126-0-9
1. Study skills. 2. Learning, Psychology of.
3. Cognitive styles. I. Title.

Book cover design & Art Direction by Susan Rouzie, Talent, Oregon
Book editing by Shanti Einolander
Book production by Great Graphics Services, Medford, Oregon
Printed in the United States of America

Endorsements

You *Are Smarter than You Think!* is a learning styles program that I have used with nursing students for the past 15 or more years. It is a program that diagnoses an individual's personal learning style, and then offers solutions for ways to enhance learning.

A lot of times when people study, they study in such a way that information is quickly lost because it is stored in their short term memory. They are cramming and able to remember information for only a short time. When students learn their appropriate learning style and subsequent methods for studying, it can allow them to study in a more effective way to retain the information over a longer period of time because information is put into long term memory. This program provides this solution as well as offering students information about the best way for them to take in information in a classroom setting as well as to interact with written information.

At Villanova University, we test the students in their freshmen year. The students often find it fun to learn about themselves. Over the many years that I have used this program with students, I have found that if the students use it as planned, they can have much greater satisfaction in learning, spend less time studying, and remember information for a much longer period of time. This creates less academic stress and a greater self esteem- all of which lead to a better college experience!

Colleen Meakim

Director, Learning Resource Center

Colleen H. Meakim, MSN, RN

Director, Learning Resource Center

Villanova University College of Nursing

It is a pleasure to put to paper a few words about such an incredible book! As an educator and former Department Chair of an Associate Degree Nursing program, I can definitely attest to the life changing attitude that can happen with a student who embraces the philosophy of " **You** *Are Smarter Than You Think!*"

I didn't know I had an option to study differently. This system has cut my study time in half and has made taking tests easier.
> Bill J.
> College Student

This learning system helped me understand my strengths and weaknesses so that I could adapt to them.
> Nan L.
> College Student

We started using this book on a volunteer basis with students, and by word of mouth the classes became so large we offered them to all nursing students. The pros of using this book are many. I have seen students go from pushing a C to an A with the study techniques and classroom activities. It is truly amazing when the "marriage" of how a student learns best is partnered with the availability of a book that shows them how to use that intelligence.

Renée Mollan-Masters, you have truly made a difference in many students' lives, and that is a wonderful legacy!

Dr. Jane C. Brenden

Mississippi Gulf Coast Community College

What impresses me most about **You** Are Smarter Than You Think!, apart from the assessments themselves and Mollan-Masters' explanation of how to use the information they provide, is the author's deep understanding of how struggling students think about learning. "The system" conditions them to believe that when conventional reading, note-taking, and study strategies (i.e. the ones used by visual/linguistic learners) don't work for them, the only way to improve is to "try harder." Paradoxically, struggling students are often so invested in these familiar strategies that they're unwilling to risk trying unfamiliar ones, especially those promising better results in less time. Mollan-Masters acknowledges this unwillingness with great sensitivity, along with the fear and anger that can accompany it, and shows learners how to validate their assessment results quickly and meaningfully.

Most of the students I work with have some idea of their gifts for receiving, reorganizing, and retaining information but have little idea of how or why to use those gifts. In their exit essays, many of my students have written about how Mollan-Masters' book has empowered them to own and use their gifts not only in academic contexts, but in professional and personal ones as well. Several have told me it has changed their lives. Simply put, this book is a gift, and I can't imagine teaching university studies without it.

Gregg Heinrichs

Coordinated Student Advising Team

University Studies

Eastern Michigan University

At Waukesha County Technical College we use **You** *Are Smarter Than You Think!* to improve the academic productivity, effectiveness and efficiency of our adult students. Our adult students come to us for several reasons. Our Supervisory / Management associate degree give many the opportunity for promotions in their existing career. Others seek new careers in the field of management. Others use the associate as a stepping-stone to a university bachelor degree. More recently, because of the 2007/8 recession, many need complete retraining for new fields and careers.

You *Are Smarter Than You Think!* provides the student and college instructor an analysis of everyone's academic learning strengths and weaknesses. `The student can now change their study, reading, team activities and test taking behaviors to be more productive and effective. The college instructor can now change their new material delivery methods to present material in ways that allow the students to be more successful.

We use **You** *Are Smarter Than You Think!*, as a tool for positive change. We have modified the review forms at the end of the book into "change contracts". After the students complete the forms they are asked to present and explain how they are going to positively change their academic behavior to improve their learning of new material.

James J. Zander

Instructor

Waukesha County Technical College

Dedication

This book is lovingly dedicated to my husband and best friend, Jerry Masters.

Contents

Acknowledgements

For the past 25 years this book has always taken me on wonderful journeys. Writing this 3rd edition was no different. Everything began with the prompting of my dear friend of over 30 years, Paul Deputy. He informed me that a facelift would make this book more acceptable to schools today. So I called another dear friend Shanti Einolander, an editor, to see how she could help. She began reading my book and making wonderful editing changes. Changes that I believe will make this edition more "user" friendly. Then Shanti told me about her friend Susan Rouzie who has done book covers for years along with other marketing projects. Susan and I met and decided to work together. About the same time I was called by an instructor at Eastern Michigan University wanting more information about my book. I was reminded that another instructor at this University used my book and so I decided to call Gregg Heinrichs to see if he had any thoughts about what should be included in the face lift. He told me that the YASTYT book was the missing piece to student success. He said most students have 90% of what they need to be successful but my book is the final piece that puts things all together. This was a new idea for me and I immediately called my cover designer and asked her to incorporate this idea into the cover.

A few days later Susan, the cover designer and I met. Her first design was the one that I chose. It is not what I thought I would choose. I thought it would be prettier. But I showed this design to a student working in the coffee shop where we met and he liked it but wanted more information on the cover so an expanded subtitle was added. Thus the cover was created. It fell into place like a magical puzzle. Susan also did the back of the cover and her ideas for changing the interior are wonderful too.

About the same time that all this was happening with the cover, I talk with Todd Hobbs my Sales Rep at CDS Publications, my fulfillment center. He suggested that I talk to Roberta Great to see if she would input all the changes suggested by Shanti and Susan. Roberta was more than willing to help. She has been such a joy to work with and I think the results are spectacular.

Again my Step daughter, Karen Masters did the final proofing. What a detail oriented wonder she is. I appreciate her expertise so much. She has always been there for me and I feel very lucky indeed.

In closing I would like to thank all the instructors who have used this book over the many years. Their support and ideas have always made this a better book and system for the student. Without them this book would have never happen. I would also like to thank, once again, the heavenly presence that has been with me guiding me since the beginning. It feels good to know that I have never been alone.

Preface

A BIRTH

About 25 years ago while I was doing research for a television show on parenting, I ran across some work done by Dr. Howard Gardner, a research scientist from Harvard University and author of the book, *Frames of Mind.*[1] This research focused on the unacknowledged talents and intellectual abilities of normal people. When I first read Dr. Gardner's work, I knew he was saying something profound. He was answering questions I had had about myself for a very long time. Questions like, why had I suddenly become *smart* in college when in high school, learning had been a constant struggle.

As life would have it, the parenting show was never produced, but during this time, I felt compelled to share Dr. Gardner's work with some local college students. These experiences with the students led directly to the creation of a learning module based on Dr. Gardner's work. For almost 22 years, this module has been successfully transforming the academic performance of students nationally.

HOW IT HAPPENED

Sound amazing? Well, this is how it all happened. For much of my life, school and learning had been difficult for me. Inside, I knew I was intelligent, but I had to work very hard for every passing grade. As a child, my older brother was able to grasp and comprehend math concepts way beyond his years. I had difficulties just understanding the basics. Yet, when it came to solving the everyday problems of life, I was the whiz and my brother was somewhat— inept. My family considered him brilliant. I was considered just average. Somehow this seemed neither fair nor *accurate*.

During my high school years, I would study the same way my friends were studying except that I would put in considerably more hours. They would get the A's and I would get the C's. This, too, seemed unfair and confusing. I had put in more time but I hadn't reaped the rewards.

LEARNING FINALLY CHANGED

Learning finally changed for me in college when I began studying speech pathology. Overnight, I became brilliant. I was learning

---

1 Howard Gardner, Frames of Mind: The Theory of Multiple Intelligences (Basic Books: A division of Harper Collins Publishers, Inc, 1983)

Our deepest fear is not that we are inadequate. Our deepest fear is that we are powerful beyond measure. It is our light, not our darkness, that most frightens us.

We ask ourselves, "Who am I to be brilliant, gorgeous, talented and fabulous?" Actually, who are you not to be?

You are a child of God. Your playing small doesn't serve the world. There's nothing enlightened about shrinking so that other people won't feel insecure around you. We were born to make manifest the glory of God that is within us.

It's not just in some of us: It's in everyone. And as we let our own light shine, we unconsciously give other people permission to do the same. As we are liberated from our own fear, our presence automatically liberates others.

Marianne Williamson
*Presented by Nelson Mandella
1994 Inaugural Speech*

almost instantly. I graduated with honors. I had no explanation for this change but was not about to question my luck.

After receiving my master's degree I then worked for 10 years with children who had language and learning problems. One of the points that was always emphasized in working with these children was the importance of teaching them *through their strengths*. Little did I know how significant this concept was to all learners.

A SOLUTION

Then came the parenting show and the discovery of Dr. Gardner's book. After reading his research, the above experiences suddenly began to assimilate. For the first time, I understood why I was able to learn so effectively in college. More importantly, however, I also understood why *before* then, learning had been so difficult for me and so easy for my friends and my brother. It was not a matter of intelligence. They were using their brains the way they were designed to be used and I was not.

STUDENT FACTOR

I began talking to the local college students about my discoveries related to Dr. Gardner's work. In the course of teaching this new information to the students, they began to apply it to their own studies. They were exuberant about their improved academic results. It was the students who encouraged me to take Dr. Gardner's work a step further and as a result, the learning system, **You** *Are Smarter Than You Think!*, was born.

THE CORE

The core of this system revolves around the idea that we all learn differently and that intelligence is really expressed in many ways. My work has shown that if we can discover where our individual abilities lie and then learn through those abilities, learning will take place more effectively than ever before.

Much of the learning that occurs in undergraduate courses isn't learning at all. It is information regurgitation. The **You** *Are Smarter Than You Think!* learning system takes learning to a new level where knowledge becomes usable and applicable beyond the test.

My desire for those of you using this book is that you too will discover that you are a whole lot smarter than you ever imagined. The doorway to your brain is about to open. Enjoy the experience!

Introduction
Is this really for me?

You are probably asking yourself, "Why do I need this book?" Well, maybe you don't. Consider the following questions and find out:

1. If you were given a comprehensive test today on material that you learned last semester, would you get a lower grade than you received originally?

2. Do you have the feeling that you are a lot smarter than your efforts and grades indicate?

3. Do you succeed in getting A's or B's but find you have to work very hard for them?

4. Do you spend hours studying and then perform poorly on tests?

5. When reading a textbook, do you often reread the material because you find it hard to remember?

6. Would you like to save twenty minutes for every hour you study?

If you answered "yes" to any of these questions, there is a very good possibility that this book will make a difference for you. Students who have used the **You** *Are Smarter Than You Think!* learning system tell us that the following benefits have occurred for them:

- Their grades improved (when improvement was possible);

- They spent less time studying—it usually drops by one-third;

- They were able to remember the material learned for longer periods of time;

- They experienced less academic stress;

- They felt better about themselves.

PLEASE NOTE . . .
Once you determine your personal learning style, you will only need to read about one-third of this book.

This system has helped me maintain my already good academic status. In addition, I am studying less, remembering what I learned for longer periods of time, and have an enhanced positive academic experience.

-Pennsylvania
Nursing Student

Would you like to enjoy these benefits?

YES, BUT I DON'T HAVE TIME

Some of you may be thinking, "It sounds great but I just don't have the time to read this book." Let me assure you that you will be reading only about one-third of this book (50 pages). The other two-thirds apply to readers with different learning styles than yours. In addition, many of the pages have pictures and other such things that require little reading.

IT AIN'T BROKE, SO DON'T FIX IT

You may also be thinking that because you are being asked to read this book, your instructors think there is something wrong with you. This is not the case at all. Teachers just know that different situations require different kinds of learning. They want you to have the greatest possible chance for success with the least amount of stress.

NOT ALL LEARNING IS THE SAME

Different types of situations require different skills. What worked for you in your undergraduate studies will probably not work for you in nursing, law, or graduate school. These programs require you to think and learn information at a much deeper level of understanding.

My nephew tells a story of his first experience in graduate school. Previously he had always been a straight A student whose study technique consisted of memorizing everything the night before each test. He used this same technique for his first test in graduate school. He was shocked when he began reading the test questions. The instructors were asking him to apply and interpret the information he had memorized the night before. He did the best he could and felt lucky to have gotten a C grade. He was shaken by this experience. He knew immediately that graduate school was a different game. What had worked previously was not going to work now.

I'll bet that most of you reading this book have been memorizing and that means you have been using your brain contrary to the way it was designed to be used. That is why you are not remembering what you learned much beyond the test or why your grades are lower than what you would like.

This book is dedicated to the idea that we are all a lot smarter than we think we are. Some of you have little faith in yourself as a learner. Your self-esteem is below where it could be. Others of you have been very successful at passing tests but remember little after the test is over. Take heart, because the **You** Are Smarter Than You Think! (**YASTYT**) book is going to change all that.

I am learning so much faster now that I am not memorizing and the information is permanent.

-Pennsylvania
Nursing Student

This program contributed to my self-esteem. This was important as I was beginning something so competitive as nursing.

-Michigan
Nursing Student

HOW TO USE THIS BOOK

Since you will only be reading about one-third of this book, you can join others who have said this can be done over a weekend.

If you have already glanced through the book, you may have noticed that many of the pages are coded with icons. These icons identify the various types of learning attributes. Once you discover which attributes are yours, you will only read those pages which apply to you. However, everyone is to read all the pages without icons. I call them the *white pages*.

The **You** *Are Smarter Than You Think!* book is broken into eight chapters, plus several appendixes. As I have said, you will not be reading every page of each chapter. It is, however, important that you read each chapter in sequence. In the first chapter called *Background— How this system works*, you will be given an understanding of this learning system. In Chapter 2, *Self-evaluation—Discovering your personal learning style*, you will take a series of personal inventories to discover not only where your brain attributes lie, but also how you process language best. In Chapter 3, 4 and 5, *How to apply your reception attribute, your reorganization attribute, and your retention attribute*, I will show you how to use these abilities to transform any learning situation into a winning situation. In Chapter 6, *A model for implementing this program*, you will learn how to gradually use this program and insure your success. In Chapter 7, *Confronting test anxiety—head-on*, you will learn how to enjoy test taking. (I kid you not!) And finally, in Chapter 8, the *Conclusion— Making a difference*, you will discover a surprise that will warm your heart and encourage your soul. (You may not go there now.) In the *Appendixes*, you will find the Tie Chart and the *Application Chart*, which you will learn about later. A note to instructors can be found there also.

Throughout this book, you will notice comments which I have collected over the years from students like yourself. I hope you will find encouragement from their experiences.

YOU ARE ON YOUR WAY

There is nothing quite like real learning. It utilizes the best of who we are. When you know that you know something, it feels very different from having just memorized it. If you are sincere about wanting to learn more effectively and are willing to do as this book instructs, a new level of achievement will open up to you. You will have the tools necessary to produce the results many of you have always wished for.

My academic experience prior to reading the **YASTYT** *book, was extremely stressful. I was brought up to believe I must always achieve the highest grade possible. Now I am learning for myself. Consequently, I don't feel as stressed.*

-Ohio
Nursing Student

Your book, **You** *Are Smarter Than You Think! is worth its weight in gold!*

John Gaddis, PhD

A NOTE TO THE LIBRARY USER

If you have checked out this book from the library, you are a library book user. As you read, you will find several places which instruct you *to write on pages.* Since this is not your book, please do not follow these instructions. Instead, you have my permission to hand copy any such section. The questions in the *Self Evaluation* chapter can be answered on a blank sheet of paper.

Please respect other users. It is rare to have permission to hand copy parts of a book. Remember, this only applies to library book use.

Background
How this system works

*Knowledge once gained casts a light beyond
its own immediate boundaries.*
—Tyndall

This is the beginning of your journey. This journey is about empowerment and honoring the best of who you are. This chapter will help you to more fully understand the theory behind this learning system so that you will be able to trust and use it later on.

When your great-grandparents were first exposed to the gasoline-burning car, they had to have some assurance that the contraption wasn't going to blow them apart the first time they stepped on the pedal. They may not have understood the complexities of the internal combustion engine, but what they did know helped them to trust the automobile and eventually buy it in great numbers.

The purpose in knowing how this system works is so that you will trust it and eventually use it. For best results, try to assimilate this background information as fully as possible. It will help you later to understand the *why* behind the techniques you will be using.

WHAT IS LEARNING?
Learning is something that occurs very naturally in life. As little children, we learn to walk and talk effortlessly. Yet, when we leave toddlerhood and enter school, things often change. Why is that?

The answer, in part, has something to do with the way in which learning takes place. As toddlers, we determine, much of the time, our learning environment. It is unstructured yet full of play and exploration. We move freely from object to object, experiencing whatever we find stimulating in that moment, and we learn. (See P*hoto A*, courtesy of Grace Christian School, Medford, OR.)

In school, however, the environment is determined for us. It is structured and often very much removed from the environment we flourished in as toddlers. (See *Photo B*, courtesy Mr. & Mrs. Don Young.)

Photo A

Photo B

Figure 1

It was enlightening to find out exactly how I learn best, so that I can focus on just those techniques.

-Wisconsin
Nursing Student

This system enables me to feel OK about using any system. In other words, it was nice to be assured that I can learn my own way and not someone else's way.

-Washington
Sociology Student

HOW I LEARN IS DIFFERENT FROM HOW YOU LEARN

It is important to understand that we all learn very differently. According to Dr. Dan Weinberger, Neurologist and Psychiatrist at the National Institute of Mental Health, "Brains normally differ more from one another than do finger prints." (*See Figure 1)*

All human beings possess their own individualized, multimillion dollar computer sitting atop their shoulders. Unfortunately, most of us do not know how to use this computer. However, as toddlers, we were successful at learning because we did use our computers correctly. This happened quite by accident through our unstructured play. We did what we enjoyed. When we entered school, we abandoned what had worked for us and instead, did what was expected.

THERE IS LEARNING AND THEN THERE IS LEARNING

Much of the learning that takes place in high school and college is unproductive. It may produce an A, but it is not *real* learning. It utilizes short-term memory and is retained just long enough to pass the test.

A STUDY

Researchers at Johns Hopkins University, Massachusetts Institute of Technology (M.I.T.), and other well-regarded universities have documented that students who receive honor grades in college-level physics courses are frequently unable to solve basic problems and questions encountered in a form slightly different from that on which they have been formally instructed and tested. (Taken from the book, *The Unschooled Mind,*[2] by Dr. Howard Gardner.)

Perhaps your instructors are asking you to read this book, not because you haven't done well in school, but rather because the kind of learning that you have done in the past will not serve you in your present situation. This is true of nursing students and law students, as well as graduate students. The learning required in these arenas is very different from the learning required elsewhere.

It utilizes long-term memory. What is being learned is associated with previously learned information. It has meaning and significance and stays with the individual long after the information is needed. Long-term memory is the basic tool for critical thinking.

2 Howard Gardner, *The Unschooled Mind: How Children Think and Schools Should Teach,* (New York: Basic Books: A division of Harper Collins Publishers Inc., 1991)

WE HAVE ALL EXPERIENCED THIS KIND OF LEARNING

Long-term learning occurs within everybody from time to time. It happens because we accidentally use our brain the way it is designed to be used. The football player who flunked biology and learned 101 complex football plays in the same semester and the high school dropout who learns the words to songs after hearing them only one time are good examples of using your brain the way it is designed. If a mind is *Musical*, it needs rhythm to learn efficiently, not words.

You may remember a time when you learned a person's address after hearing it only once. Or maybe you remember a time when you learned someone's name easily instead of struggling with it. In both of these examples, you didn't suddenly get smarter, you just used your brain correctly.

INTELLIGENCE IS MORE THAN YOU THINK

I didn't fully understand the significance of this phenomenon until several years ago when reading the book, *Frames of Mind*, by Dr. Howard Gardner, a researcher at Harvard University. Through his analysis of learning styles, Dr. Gardner has blown a hole in the traditional definition of intelligence. He maintains that all normal human beings possess seven areas of intelligence. Traditional IQ tests have focused only on two of these areas and he believes that the other five areas deserve more attention.

I agree with Dr. Gardner. As a matter of fact, I have discovered that most human beings have abilities or talents in several of these seven areas and that long-term learning takes place when these areas of talent are stimulated.

Before I explain, I want you to understand that this explanation is done from an experiential point of view and is not yet verified scientifically. It is an explanation which has been found to be helpful by those learning this system and should be used only for that purpose.

Within our brain, we have areas of short-term memory and long-term memory. Seven neurological pathways lead into these areas like freeways going to a ballpark. Some of these pathways look like the ones in *Figure 2*. They go from hither to yon and back again.

Have you ever tried to learn something and found it necessary to review the material again and again before you were able to remember it? Well, you were probably using a pathway that looks like our example in *Figure 2*.

Still other pathways look like the ones in *Figure 3*. The pathways have actual breaks in them.

This system helped me with my grades. It cut my study time and I really know the material instead of it just being memorized.

-Washington
Business Major

THE BRAIN

Legend
ST — short-term memory
LT — long-term memory

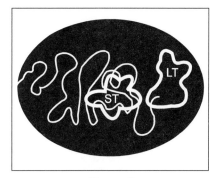

Figure 2

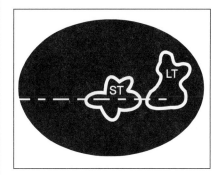

Figure 3

Figure 4

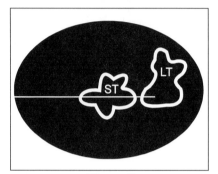

Figure 5

I went from a C in microbiology to an A on my last test and I still remember everything.

-Pennsylvania
Nursing Student

You may remember a time when you thought you had learned something and then the next day when you tried to recall what you had learned, you couldn't remember a thing. Probably you used a pathway like the one in *Figure 3*.

Other pathways look like the one in *Figure 4*. They are poorly insulated, so they short out, similar to how the wiring in a house might short out if it isn't insulated properly.

Have you ever experienced a time when, before a test, you knew everything. During the test you couldn't remember a thing. But after the test, when you relaxed, all the information came flooding back to you? Your circuits probably shorted out when stress was present and began functioning again when the stress was alleviated.

Fortunately, all normal human beings have two or three neurological pathways that look like the ones in *Figure 5*. They are strong and well developed and can carry information effectively.

THE KEY IS HOW YOU PROCESS IT

When a stimulus, such as a person's name, jumps onto one of these beautiful thoroughfares, you will remember that person's name for a long time, and learning will be almost instantaneous. This happens because the stimulus goes directly to long-term memory. However, if a similar stimulus jumps onto one of the neurological channels that is not very well developed, as previously illustrated, you will forget the name almost instantly or hold it only for a few minutes or seconds, and then forget it because the stimulus only gets to short-term memory.

Your intelligence, or rather your ability to learn, has not changed in either situation. The only thing that has been altered is the way in that you processed the incoming stimulus. One way worked and the other way didn't. The reason I suddenly had success in graduate school wasn't because I instantly became smarter. It occurred because I accidentally began learning through a neurological pathway which was well developed. I am, according to Dr. Gardner's model, talented in *Knowing Others*. People who are talented in *Knowing Others* learn better through doing than by reading a book. Those who fall into this category are *Experiential Learners*. When I began studying speech pathology, I would learn about a certain speech disability in class and then go into the clinic and work with clients who had these same problems. Working one-on-one with these clients allowed me to experience the specifics of what had been discussed in class and thus, long-term learning occurred.

THE IDEA WAS BORN

When I first read Dr. Gardner's work, the thought occurred to me that anyone, not just me, who discovered his or her attributes and stimulated those corresponding neurological pathways during learning, would also learn more effectively.

I began trying this idea with college students. I will never forget the day I knew I was on to something. I was walking across campus and someone came up to me from behind, grabbed me, and shouted, "It works." I thought I was being attacked. Instead, an excited student was reporting to me that a miracle had occurred in her life.

Only the day before, this student had discovered that she was talented *Musically* and *Body Kinesthetically*—two of Dr. Gardner's channels. She informed me that she played the piano by ear. She also mentioned that she had an anatomy test coming up, for which she had to learn a great number of anatomical terms. I suggested that she put this information on a tape—for reasons I will discuss later—then listen to the tape while she played the piano. Playing the piano is not only a *Musical* ability, but also a *Body Kinesthetic* (body movement) ability. She listened to the tape of terms one time through while she played the piano. She then had her parents test her on the material to see how much she had learned. To her surprise, she had learned everything on the first try.

TAPPING INTO YOUR INNATE ABILITIES

Sound unbelievable? The results happened not for any mysterious reason but simply because the student was tapping into her innate intelligence. She was stimulating her strong neurological pathways and the information was going straight to long-term memory. This is the best-case scenario. Most people will have to review the material being learned a couple of times but generally not more.

It has been believed for years that we use between 2 percent and 10 percent of our natural intelligence. I believe that when we learn how to use our brains the way they are meant to be used, a far greater percentage of our intelligence is made available to us and therefore learning improves.

When you move on to the *Self-Evaluation* chapter of this book, keep in mind what has been discussed above. Remember, all people of normal intelligence who have not experienced brain damage have areas of talent. You may not be manifesting these abilities, but the neurological pathways still exist and can be used quite effectively to facilitate your learning.

It is a good feeling to walk into a testing situation when you are confident and feel you've got a handle on all the materials being tested. That is what this system did for me.

-Pennsylvania
Nursing Student

YASTYT *has helped me tremendously. In fact, I didn't use the techniques I learned from this book on a recent test and my grades showed it. It made me realize just how effective it is.*

-Pennsylvania
Nursing Student

I sleep better before exams. This system is so much better than just memorizing.

-Pennsylvania
Nursing Student

This program helped me know myself better.

-Pennsylvania
Psychology Major

I like studying and maintaining good grades. Using this system has helped me study more efficiently.

-So. California
Nursing Student

Figure 6

ARE YOU AN AUDITORY, VISUAL, OR COMBINATION LANGUAGE PROCESSOR?

What skill do you think people use most when they are in school: visual memory, language processing, or verbal expression? The answer is *language processing*. If you look at all the activities you do in a single day as a student, you will see that many of these activities center around language processing.

So what is language processing? If you observe an accident and can tell the police exactly what happened, this is *not* language processing. However, when you read a book or listen to someone else talking, you are processing language.

Let's list all the things we do as students:

- Listen to lectures—This is language processing.
- Read text books—This is language processing.
- Take tests—This is language processing.
- Study for tests—This is language processing.
- Write a paper—Some elements involve language processing.

MOST EVERYONE HAS A PREFERENCE

When I was developing this program, I wondered if normal learners have a preference for how they process language. Do some people remember more if they hear the information, while others remember more if they read it? What I discovered, after surveying thousands of students, surprised me. People usually do have a preference and having a preference is normal.

Some people have perfectly normal hearing, yet they have a great deal of difficulty remembering what they have heard. Many times these people are considered poor listeners, when in reality, they listen and hear well. What they hear just doesn't sink in. (*See figure 6*)

Other people, with normal vision or vision which has been corrected, have a difficult time remembering what they have read. They may be great readers, but when their reading comprehension is checked, it is usually poor.

Some people have difficulties processing language with their eyes and their ears separately, but when language is processed through both their eyes and ears together, e.g., reading aloud, then comprehension is very good. We call these people *Combination Language Processors.*

KNOWING YOUR PREFERENCE IS IMPORTANT

Knowing your preference is very important if you are interested in learning more effectively. It fits hand-in-hand with Dr. Gardner's learning style information which I discussed earlier. If the information you want to learn isn't getting into the system, it doesn't matter how your brain is functioning, because there is nothing there to process. Many of you will be surprised to learn just how little information is getting in when you read or listen.

We are now ready to move on to the *Self-Evaluation* chapter of this book. This chapter will help you to uncover your strengths in terms of Dr. Gardner's model, as well as your preference for processing language. It is important to remember that we are all beautifully different. The key is to discover your strengths and run with them. Everybody has areas of weakness. It is normal. In *Photograph C*, to the right, you see Tim Milton, skiing at Mt. Ashland, Oregon. Tim is a young man who is blind, and yet he skis. Winners focus on their strengths and don't worry about their shortcomings. Read on and have fun discovering what makes you tick. (Photo courtesy of Mr. and Mrs. Wes Milton.)

Knowing how I learn best makes me feel more comfortable.

Photograph C

Self-Evaluation
Discovering your personal learning style

The sun has one kind of splendor, the moon another and the stars another.
—I Corinthians 15:41

DISCOVERING YOUR PERSONAL LEARNING STYLE

Like everything else in this universe, you too have your own kind of splendor. We are now going to discover how your particular splendor shines. We will do this by helping you discover two things about yourself. The first will be where your gifts lie in terms of Howard Gardner's model. The second will be how you process language best.

Dr. Gardner's research tells us that we all have areas of strength. The trick is to discover our strengths and use them to our advantage. You are now going to take an inventory that will help you discover where your natural abilities lie, so that later you can use these abilities to learn more effectively.

CHILDREN ARE MORE HONEST ABOUT THEMSELVES

As children, we are very honest about who we are. As we mature, we sometimes hide our best attributes because they do not seem acceptable in our eyes or in society's eyes. A number of years ago a student of mine discovered that she was very talented physically. She remembered being very good at sports as a child, but as an adult, she never did anything physical. Many talents that are innately ours become buried as adults. For example, you may have been very Musical as a child but as an adult, music may play a very small role in your life. The important thing to know is, that even if you are not very Musical now, but you were as a child, this pathway is still intact and can be used to your advantage.

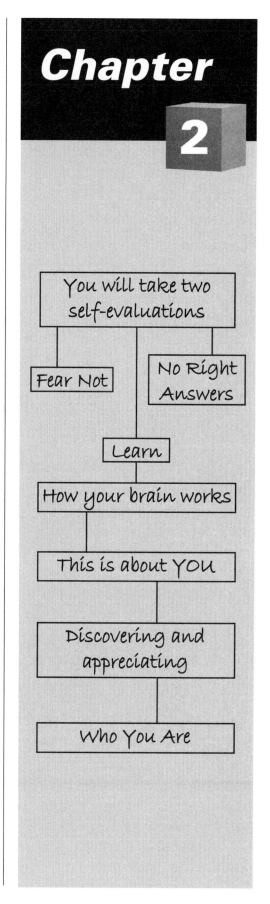

Chapter 2

You will take two self-evaluations

Fear Not

No Right Answers

Learn

How your brain works

This is about YOU

Discovering and appreciating

Who You Are

Self-Evaluation-Part1

We have created an inventory based on Dr. Howard Gardner's styles of learning. It asks you about yourself now, as well as when you were a child. Some of you may honestly not remember these aspects of your childhood. This is fine. If you cannot recall a certain childhood situation, leave the question blank. However, you may find that you do remember other childhood situations. Answer those questions.

The correct way to take this inventory is to read each question and go with your first impulse. You will be surprised at how accurate your responses will be. Don't do a great deal of thinking.

Read each question carefully. Then read each attribute under the question. Next quickly decide which attribute or attributes sound most like you. Do this on all the questions. Lastly, check the corresponding box or boxes on the answer sheet next to the questions. For some of the questions you will have more than one answer and for others you may have no answer.

EXAMPLE

On the facing page you will see a list of questions and an answer sheet. On the answer sheet you will see numbers, letters, white boxes and gray boxes. Ignore the gray boxes. Now read question number one. Then read the A, B, and C attributes under the same question. Decide which attribute(s) sound most like you. Next look at the answer sheet. If the A attribute sounds most like you put a check mark in the A box next to number one. If the B attribute sound most like you put a check mark in the B box next to number one and so on. Remember, you may have more than one check mark per question or no check mark at all.

As you read through the survey you may notice that the letters of the alphabet are not sequential. Don't worry about this. It has been set up this way to make scoring easier.

Move through this section quickly. Go with your first impulse, but be sure to read each question accurately. Trust yourself. Trust your responses and have fun.

You may now begin.

Understanding what works makes studying less stressful.

-So. California
Nursing Student

I used to get sick, and sweat before a test. Now I don't experience any of these problems.

-Washington
Student

YOUR PERSONAL LEARNING INVENTORY

1. When you were a child . . .

    (A) —You talked very early and never shut up. You may remember a certain irritability from adults towards your talking.

    (B) —You liked to eat your foods separately—first your potatoes and then your vegetables, and finally your meat.

    (C) —You loved coloring.

2. Of the following, check the ones that seem most like you.

    (A) —It irritates you when people use the wrong word to describe something.

    (B) —If your work area has been messed up by someone else, this upsets you and you must clean it up before you can be OK again.

    (C) —If you stood in the middle of the street in front of where you are now sitting, you could point out north, south, east and west.

3. When you were a child . . .

    (D) —You were often distracted by environmental sounds, such as the gnats hitting the window or the buzz in the refrigerator.

    (E) —You learned to tie your shoelaces and ride a bike easily.

    (F) —You were a good judge of what you could and could not do (you were adventuresome).

    (G) —You enjoyed making up plays and acting out roles.

4. Of the following, check the ones that seem most like you.

    (D) —You hear rhythm in environmental sounds.

    (E) —You find it difficult to sit still for long periods of time.

    (F) —You would enjoy being in a play.

    (G) —You consider yourself to be a good judge of people.

Page 11 - Answer Sheet

	A	B	C	D	E	F	G
1							
2							
3							
4							
SUB-TOTAL							

Page 12 - Answer Sheet

	A	B	C	D	E	F	G
5							
6							
7							
8							
9							
SUB-TOTAL							

5. When you were a child . . .

    (A) —you read before you started school and/or were one of the better readers in class.

    (B) —in your room or special area, you liked to categorize your things: your toys, your clothes or your collections.

    (C) —when reading a book, the pictures were more important than the words.

6. Of the following, check the ones that seem most like you.

    (A) —Reading the directions is more helpful than looking at the diagrams without reading the directions.

    (B) —If you are honest with yourself, down deep, you believe that there is usually one best way to do something.

    (C) —You can draw maps or pictures well and/or are good at photography and/or enjoy doing crafts.

7. When you were a child . . .

    (D) —you enjoyed listening to music.

    (E) —you imitated the funny movements and expressions of people you saw.

    (F) —you enjoyed making up plays and acting out roles.
    (G) —you read people easily. You could tell when someone was lying, or if they were good, bad, or safe.

8. Of the following, check the ones that seem most like you.

    (D) —You can sing on key and/or play a musical instrument.

    (E) —Physical exercise makes you feel good.

    (F) —You are very particular about what you eat and what you wear.

    (G) —You learn better by doing something rather than by reading about it.

9. When you were a child . . .

    (A) —you were a good storyteller, and/or you were able to express yourself well with your writing.

    (B) —you often asked questions such as, How does thunder and lightning work? What makes it rain? When did time begin?

    (C) —you never got lost. You had a good sense of direction.

10. Of the following, check the ones that seem most like you.

(A) —You love words.

(B) —Textbook material often seems poorly organized.

(C) —When reading textbook material, you find yourself becoming confused by the abundance of words being used.

11. Of the following, check the ones that seem most like you.

(D) —Certain types of music calm and soothe you.

(E) —You are good at and enjoy at least one of the following:

> sports
>
> outdoor games
>
> dancing

(F) —You are good at knowing if you will do well on a test.

(G) —You find yourself being the mediator for friends and family.

12. Of the following, check the ones that seem most like you.

(D) —When music is playing, often your foot is also tapping.

(E) —You express excitement with your whole body.

(F) —If asked what you are feeling right now, you could tell me in detail.

(G) —You like playing characters in plays.

13. When you were a child . . .

(A) —you learned poems and/or radio and TV jingles easily (the words, not the music).

(B) —you know exactly where something is even though your space may be a mess.

(C) —school academics was not easy.

14. Which of the following sounds most like you?

(A) —You love to tell jokes and stories and you tell them well.

(B) —You prefer things to be sequentially organized.

(C) —If someone was giving you directions to their house, you would prefer a drawing over written out directions.

Page 13 - Answer Sheet

	A	B	C	D	E	F	G
10							
11							
12							
13							
14							
SUB-TOTAL							

Page 14 - Answer Sheet

	A	B	C	D	E	F	G
15							
16							
17							
18							
SUB-TOTAL							

15. When you were a child . . .
    (D) —you could distinguish between the sirens of a fire truck, a police car, and an ambulance.

    (E) —you enjoyed recess.

    (F) —you knew definitely what you wanted to eat or wear even if you were not allowed to make those choices.

    (G) —when someone was introduced to you for the first time, you sometimes would say, "She reminds me of so and so."

16. When you were a child . . .
    (D) —you could do one or more of the following: read musical notes, play an instrument, sing by ear.

    (E) —you found it difficult to sit still in school for long periods of time.

    (F) —you connected actions with feelings and said or thought, "I did it because I was mad," after doing something inappropriate.

    (G) —if someone showed you how to do something, you could then do it easily.

17. Of the following, check the ones that seem most like you.
    (A) —You love to read.

    (B) —It is difficult for you to follow a conversation when the speakers jump around from subject to subject.

    (C) —During a conversation you really don't mind if the speakers jump around from subject to subject, as long as you know the bottom line.

18. Of the following, check the ones that seem most like you.
    (D) —One of your favorite things to do is to go to a concert and/or musical comedy.

    (E) —If you had a choice between watching TV or doing something active, you most generally would opt for something physical.

    (F) —When you teach someone something, you find that you learn it at a deeper level.

    (G) —You are good at identifying the core issue of a problem.

GRAND TOTAL ANSWER SHEET

	ATTRIBUTE A	ATTRIBUTE B	ATTRIBUTE C	ATTRIBUTE D	ATTRIBUTE E	ATTRIBUTE F	ATTRIBUTE G
Sub-totals Page 11							
Sub-totals Page 12							
Sub-totals Page 13							
Sub-totals Page 14							
GRAND TOTAL							

SCORING DIRECTIONS

1. *Transfer* all your sub-totals from the previous pages to the chart on this page.

2. *Add* down each column and put these numbers in the grand total box below each column. When you finish you should have a grand total number for attributes A through G. (Some boxes may have a score of zero.)

3. Now look at your *Personal Learning Summary* chart which will you find on the next page. Put your name and date at the top. (Disregard the *Reception* section for the moment.) Look halfway down the *Summary* and you will see the *Reorganization* and *Retention* sections. Record the scores from the *Grand Total Answer Sheet* on this page, to the *lines* opposite the corresponding attributes.

Example: If you got a score of 4 on *Attribute* A on the *Grand Total Answer Sheet*, you would put a 4 on the line *after* *Attribute* A—*Linguistic*, on the *Personal Learning Summary chart*. Be sure to record all scores for all attributes.

My Personal Learning Summary
Success Map *(Tear this page out.)*

Name _____   Date _____

RECEPTION	page 43	Score	
Auditory Language Processor		_____	_____
Visual Language Processor		_____	_____
Combination Language Processor		_____	_____

REORGANIZATION	page 57	Score	
Attribute A - Linguistic		_____	_____
Attribute B - Logical		_____	_____
Attribute C - Spatial		_____	_____

RETENTION	page 101	Score	
Attribute D - Musical		_____	_____
Attribute E - Body Kinesthetic		_____	_____
Attribute F - Knowing Self		_____	_____
Attribute G - Knowing Others		_____	_____

An extra copy of this form can be found in the Appendix.

Tear out along this perforated edge.

Self-Evaluation-Part 2

You are now about to learn how you process language best. As you discovered earlier, much of what you do as a student involves language processing, so discovering your preference is important. You will discover your preference for language processing by reading and listening to a selected story that has been broken into three sections.

Thousands of people have discovered their talents using this story. Don't let your own judgements get in your way. I have found that most people do not have an accurate sense about their abilities in this area. Remember, we are talking about one's ability to process language. There is a very big difference between that and remembering what something looked like.

I would also like to add that you might do very poorly in one or two sections of this activity. Don't cheat. I know that it might get uncomfortable. It is normal to have difficulties with one or more of these sections. It is also normal to not have difficulties with one or two of these sections. The skills you are uncovering, you were born with. If you respect them, they will serve you. They say nothing about your intelligence. Please remember, we are all very different, especially in how we process information, and one way is not better than any other.

Are you ready? Let's begin.

Come to the edge, he said.
They said: We are afraid.
Come to the edge, he said.
They came.
He pushed them . . .
and they flew.

Guillaume Apollinaire

ARE YOU AN AUDITORY LANGUAGE PROCESSOR?
During the first part of this section, you will discover your *Auditory Language Processing* ability. You will need to have someone read the Auditory section of this story to you. Don't look at this story please. You will be asked to answer 10 content questions after you have heard this section of the story. You must have someone read this first section to you. There is no other way. Please ask someone who will not want to participate in this activity later.

DO NOT PROCEED UNTIL YOU DO THIS!

Now that you have someone to read you the *Auditory Section*, here are the ground rules. You, the listener, must sit in a comfortable location where you can listen carefully. Do not look at the selection. Instruct the reader to read the selection to you at a normal speed. As you listen, do not take notes. Listen as though you were listening to something important. Now have your reader turn to the next page and read you the selection. When finished, turn to *Page 26* and answer the ten auditory questions and correct them as instructed.

Relax!

This is not a test.

The results from this activity have nothing to do with your intelligence.

Renée Mollan-Masters

AUDITORY SELECTION

A Rose for Miss Caroline

by Arthur Gordon

Every Saturday night, all through the lazy spring, I used to take a rose to Miss Caroline Wellford. Every Saturday night, rain or shine, at exactly eight o'clock.

It was always the best rose in the shop. I would watch Old Man Olsen nest it tenderly in green tissue paper and fern. Then I would take the narrow box and pedal furiously through the quiet street and deliver the rose to Miss Caroline. In those days, after school and on Saturdays, I worked as a delivery boy for Olsen, the florist. The job paid only three dollars a week, but that was a lot for a teenager then.

From the beginning there was something a little strange about those roses—or rather, about the circumstances under which I delivered them. The night the first one was sent I pointed out to Mr. Olsen that he had forgotten the card.

He peered at me through his glasses like a benevolent gnome. "There isn't any card, James." He never called me Jimmy. "And furthermore the—uh—party sending this flower wants it done as quietly as possible. So keep it under your hat, will you?"

I was glad Miss Caroline was getting a flower, because we all felt sorry for her. As everybody in our small town knew, the worst of all fates had befallen Miss Caroline. She had been jilted.

For years she had been as good as engaged to Jeffrey Penniman, one of the ablest young bachelors in town. She had waited while he got himself through medical school. She was still waiting when, halfway through his internship, Dr. Penniman fell in love with a younger, prettier girl and married her.

It was almost a scandal. My mother said that all men were brutes and that Jeffrey Penniman deserved to be horse-whipped. My father said, on the contrary, that it was the right—no, the sacred duty—of every man to marry the prettiest girl who would have him.

STOP

Please turn to the next page to answer questions. . .

AUDITORY QUESTIONS

Please answer the following questions after someone has read you the above selection.

(Library book users please answer these questions on a separate piece of paper.)

Do your best and don't worry if you have difficulties remembering. It is normal.

1. What time would the boy deliver the rose each week?

2. What was the rose wrapped with?

3. Who wrapped the rose?

4. How much did the boy get paid each week?

5. What was missing from the delivery?

6. What was the boy's name?

7. Who sent the flowers?

8. What happened to Miss Caroline?

9. Who had she been engaged to? (first and last name)

10. The boy's mother said that the person in number nine should be what?

Library users, please record your scores on the Learning Summary sheet you made above.

Turn to *Page 26* and correct your answers. Put a line through the numbers of the ones you miss. If you get half an answer correct, give yourself a half score for that question.

Count the number of correct answers you got and put that number on the *Auditory Score* line below. Then record that score on your *Personal Learning Summary* sheet (*Page 17*) under the Reception section where you see the words *Auditory Language Processor*.

Auditory Language Processing Score_____

When you have recorded your score in both places, move to the next section of this activity (*Page 27*).

Please turn to the next page and correct your answers . .

AUDITORY ANSWERS

1. 8:00 p.m. (If you just knew it was eight and not morning or night, give yourself half credit.)

2. Green tissue paper. (If you put tissue or paper or tissue paper or fern, give yourself half credit.)

3. Mr. Olsen or Old Man Olsen.

4. $3.00.

5. A card or note.

6. Jimmy or James. (Give yourself half credit if you put Jim.)

7. It was a secret or unknown or anonymous—anything of this nature.

8. Jilted or anything of this nature.

9. Jeffrey Penniman. (If you put Dr. Penniman, give yourself half a point. If you said Mr. Penniman, give yourself no points.)

10. Horse-whipped.

ARE YOU A VISUAL LANGUAGE PROCESSOR?

You are now ready to discover your *Visual Language Processing* abilities. On the following page you will be asked to read silently the next third of our story. DO NOT LOOK AT IT UNTIL YOU ARE READY TO BEGIN. When you are ready to begin reading, remember these ground rules:

First, read the material at your normal reading speed. Read silently.

Start at the top and read the selection one time through, completely.

Do not go back and reread any portion.

Do not write or underline as you read.

You may now begin.

VISUAL SELECTION

A Rose for Miss Caroline—continued . . .

The girl Jeffrey Penniman married was a beauty, all right. Her name was Christine Marlowe, and she came from a big city. She must have had an uncomfortable time in our town, because naturally the women despised her and said unkind things about her.

As for poor Miss Caroline, the effect on her was disastrous. For six months she had shut herself up in her house, stopped leading her Girl Scout Troop, given up all civic activities. She even refused to play the organ at church anymore.

Miss Caroline wasn't old or unhandsome, but she seemed determined to turn herself into an eccentric old maid. She looked like a ghost the night when I delivered the first rose. "Hello, Jimmy," she said listlessly. When I handed her the box, she looked startled— "For me?"

Again the next Saturday, at exactly the same time, I found myself delivering another rose to Miss Caroline. And the next Saturday yet another. The third time she opened the door so quickly that I knew she must have been waiting. There was a little color in her cheeks, now, and her hair no longer looked so straggly.

The morning after my fourth trip to her house, Miss Caroline played the organ again in church. The rose, I saw, was pinned to her blouse. She held her head high; she did not glance once at the pew where Dr. Penniman sat with his beautiful bride. What courage, my mother said, what character!

Week after week I delivered the rose and gradually Miss Caroline resumed her normal life. There was something proud about her now, something defiant almost—the attitude of a woman who may have suffered an outward defeat, but now knows inwardly that she is still cherished and loved.

The night came, eventually, when I made my final trip to Miss Caroline's house. I said, as I handed her the box, "This is the last time I'll bring this, Miss Caroline. We're moving away next week. But Mr. Olsen says he'll keep sending the flowers."

STOP

Please turn to the next page to answer questions . .

VISUAL QUESTIONS

1. Where did Mrs. Penniman come from?

2. How long had Miss Caroline shut herself up in her house?

3. What wasn't she doing with the church anymore?

4. What did Miss Caroline look like the first night Jimmy delivered a rose?

5. After the fourth rose was delivered, what did Miss Caroline resume doing?

6. What was she wearing when she did this?

7. Who did she not look at?

8. Jimmy's mom said that Miss Caroline had two things. What were they?

9. Miss Caroline reflected inward _____?

10. What was going to happen to Jimmy at the end of this section?

Turn to *Page 32* and correct your answers. Put a line through the numbers of the ones you miss. If you get half an answer correct, give yourself a half score for that question.

Count the number of correct answers you got and put that number on the *Visual Score* line below. Then record that score on your *Personal Learning Summary sheet* (*Page 17*) under the *Reception* section where you see the words *Visual Language Processor*.

Visual Language Processing Score _____

When you have recorded your score in both places, move to the next section of this activity (Page 33).

Please turn to the next page and correct your answers . .

VISUAL ANSWERS

1. A big city.

2. Six months.

3. Playing the organ.

4. A ghost—this is the only correct answer.

5. Playing the organ at church or just playing the organ.

6. The rose.

7. Dr. Penniman and his bride/wife, or Jeffrey and his wife, or Jeffrey and Christine—anything of this nature will do. If you called Dr. Penniman *Mr. Penniman* give yourself half credit. If you left either Dr. Penniman or his wife out, give yourself half credit.

8. Courage and character.

9. Love.

10. He was moving

ARE YOU A COMBINATION LANGUAGE PROCESSOR?

You are now ready to discover how you function when information enters both your ears and your eyes at the same time. In order to test this skill, you will have to read the next part of our story aloud. You may feel silly doing this but it is very important. If you must, close the door so that you can do it in private.

Don't look at the story until you are ready to read the selection aloud. When you are reading, remember that comprehending the content is more important than how you sound. Read just loud enough so that you can hear yourself. Read the entire section one time through and do not go back and read any portion twice. Make sure that you do not follow the words with your finger.

When you are ready, turn to the next page and begin reading aloud.

COMBINATION SELECTION
A Rose for Miss Caroline—continued . . .

She hesitated. Then she said, "Come in for a minute, Jimmy."

She led me into her prim sitting room. From the mantel she took a model of a sailing ship, exquisitely carved. "This was my grandfather's," she said. "I'd like you to have it. You've brought me great happiness, Jimmy—you and your roses."

She opened the box, touched the delicate petals. "They say so much, though they are silent. They speak to me of other Saturday nights, happy ones. They tell me that he, too, is lonely..." She bit her lip, as if she had said too much. "You'd better go now, Jimmy. Go!"

Clutching my ship model, I fled to my bicycle. Back at the shop, I did what I had never had the nerve to do. I looked in the file where Mr. Olsen kept his untidy records, and I found what I was looking for. "Penniman," it said, in Mr. Olsen's crabbed script. "Fifty- two American Beauties—$.25. Total: $13. Paid in advance." WELL, I thought to myself. WELL!

The years went by, and one day I came again to Olsen's flower shop. Nothing had changed. Old Man Olsen was making a corsage of gardenias, just as he used to do. We talked awhile, my old boss and I. Then I said, "Whatever became of Miss Caroline? You remember—she got the roses."

"Miss Caroline?" He nodded. "Why, she married George Halsey —owns the drugstore. Fine fellow. They have twins."

"Oh!" I said, a bit surprised. Then I decided to show Mr. Olsen how smart I had been. "D'you suppose," I said, "that Mrs. Penniman ever knew her husband was sending flowers to his old flame?"

Mr. Olsen sighed. "James, you never were very bright. Jeffrey Penniman didn't send them. He never even knew about `em."

I stared at him. "Who did, then?"

"A lady," said Mr. Olsen. He put the gardenias carefully into a box. "A lady who said she wasn't going to sit around watching Miss Caroline make a martyr of herself at her expense. Christine Penniman sent those roses."

"Now *there*," he said, closing the lid with finality, "was a woman for you!"

STOP

A Rose for Miss Caroline—Taken from Through Many Windows. Copyright 1883 by Arthur Gorden, published by Fleming H. Revell Col, Old Tappan, NJ.

Please turn to the next page to answer questions . .

COMBINATION QUESTIONS

1. Miss Caroline asked Jimmy to do what at the beginning of this section?

2. What did she take off the mantel?

3. Whose was it?

4. Who did Miss Caroline think was sending the flowers?

5. Where did Jimmy go after leaving her?

6. What did he do there?

7. When Jimmy came back years later, what was Mr. Olsen doing?

8. Who did Miss Caroline marry?

9. What did they have?

10. Who really sent the roses?

Turn to *Page 38* and correct your answers. Put a line through the numbers of the ones you miss. If you get half an answer correct, give yourself a half score for that question.

Count the number of correct answers you got and put that number on the *Combination Score* line below. Then record that score on your *Personal Learning Summary* sheet (*Page 17*) under the *Reception* section where you see the words *Combination Language Processor*.

Combination Language Processing Score _____

When you have recorded your score in both places, move to the next section of this activity (*Page 39*).

Please turn to the next page and correct your answers . .

COMBINATION ANSWERS

1. To come in.

2. A model sailing ship or a model ship or ship. (Give yourself half credit if you had any other kind of ship.)

3. Grandfather's.

4. Dr. Penniman or Jeffrey. (If you put Mr., give yourself half credit.)

5. To the shop, or Mr. Olsen's, or something of this nature.

6. Looked in the file, or looked in the records or something of this nature.

7. Making a corsage—your answer must have the word corsage in it to get credit.

8. George Halsey.

9. Twins.

10. Christine Penniman (If you got half the name correct give yourself half credit.)

NEXT . . .

Look again at your *Personal Learning Summary* sheet (*Page 17*). You should have entered all your scores from the above activities on this form. If you have not done this, please do so now.

Look at the first section, *Reception*, of your *Personal Learning Summary*. Notice that it contains the words *Auditory*, *Visual*, and *Combination Language Processor*. Now look at your scores for these three categories and circle the icon opposite the category with your highest score. Example: Let's say you got a three in *Auditory*, a five in *Visual*, and a nine in *Combination*. Your highest score is in *Combination*, so you will want to circle the ear/eye icon opposite the word *Combination*. If you have a tie or all three scores are the same, circle the two or three icons opposite your highest scores.

Next look at the section on this same form that contains the words, *Linguistic*, *Logical* and *Spatial*. Look at your scores for these three attributes and circle the icon next to the attribute in which you scored highest. Example: Let's say you have a one in *Linguistic*, a two in *Logical* and a three in *Spatial*. You will then circle the icon opposite *Spatial*, because you got your highest score in this category.

If this is your book, and if you wish, you may tear out the *Personal Learning Summary* now. Please remember to read on and finish filling out the rest of this form.

FOR A TIE

If you find you have a tie in one or more of the A, B and C attributes, you will want to see if you can break the tie. Do this by going back to pages 11-14. Reread any question that has an A, B, or C for an answer. Then look at the attributes you marked for that question. Read each attribute's description carefully and see if one of the descriptions seems more like you than the other. If it does, erase the mark on your answer sheet for the description that seems less like you. Reread all the questions with an A, B, and C answer. You may not change all answers. That is fine. Re-tally your score.

If you still have a tie after doing this, then read Chapter 4, page 57, and see which strategy seems best for you. Don't do it now. Wait until you get to that section. You may find that a combination of two of these strategies might also be an option.

NOW . . .

Look at the next section on your *Personal Learning Summary*. In this section, you will see the words *Musical*, *Body Kinesthetic*, *Knowing Self*, and *Knowing Others*. Here you

Our doubts are traitors, and make us lose the good we oft might win by fearing to attempt.

William Shakespeare

My study time has decreased with this system which then makes it possible for me to spend more time with my family.

-Wisconsin
Nursing Student

will circle two icons. Look at your scores and circle the two icons across from the attributes in which you have the highest score. Example: Let's say you got a two in *Musical*, a one in *Body Kinesthetic*, a three in *Knowing Self* and a three in *Knowing Others*. Your highest scores are in *Knowing Self* and *Knowing Others*, so you circle the icons opposite both of these attributes. If you have scores that are one point apart in this section, circle them too. Example: Let's say that you have a three in *Musical*, a five in *Body Kinesthetic*, a four in *Knowing Self* and a one in *Knowing Others*. You would circle the *Knowing Self*, *Musical*, and *Body Kinesthetic* attributes.

ANOTHER TIE?

If you have a tie in all four categories, you may want to double check and see if they are all equally strong. Do this by going back to pages 11-14. Reread any question that has a D, E, F, or G for an answer. Then look at the attributes you marked for that question. Read each attribute's description carefully and see if one of the descriptions seems more like you than the other. If it does, erase the mark on your answer sheet for the description that seems less like you. Reread all questions with a D, E, F, G answer. You may not change all answers. That is fine. Re-tally your score and your tie should be broken.

If your tie is not broken don't worry. It will be discussed more fully in Chapter 5.

BEFORE YOU GO ON . . .

Take a moment right now and look at your *Personal Learning Summary*. You have in your hands an indication of your attributes, which is your map to success. Look at all the icons you circled. They indicate your areas of strength. Focus on them. Feel good about them. Winners run with their abilities and forget their weakness.

Several years ago a young lady came to me in frustration. She had been a licensed Vocational Nurse for 20 years and wanted to become a nurse. The only problem was that she had flunked the entrance exam into the nursing program not once, but twice; and the second time she failed worse than the first. She came to me because she had heard that the **You** *Are Smarter Than You Think!* learning system had helped nursing students and she thought maybe it could help her too.

She took the evaluations just as you have taken them. We discovered her area strengths just as you have done. We focused solely on her abilities and I showed her how to study, using only those abilities. She studied this new way. She took

He who has begun his task has half done it.

Horace

the entrance exam again and not only did she pass, but she got the highest score that anyone had ever received at that school.

Like this student, you will discover how to use your newly- found abilities to learn faster and more effectively than ever before.

Reception Attribute
How to use it

*Learning and wanting to learn are inseparable.
You learn best when you believe what
you are trying to learn is of value to you.*
—A Course in Miracles

Chapter

3

*Now that you know how
your brain functions best, in
the next few chapters, you
will discover, step by step,
how to use these attributes
to transform any learning
situation into a winning
experience. In this chapter
you will learn about the
first step in this three-step
process.*

CHANGE IS A SCARY THING
Before we go on, I thought you might find it interesting to read
this perspective from one student who successfully used the
YASTYT program and was also a little resistant to the idea at first.

INSIGHT FROM A STUDENT
"My name is Debbie Gallagher. I want to share an experience
with you in hopes that it may enlighten you as it did me. I tend
to be a fairly strong 'Type A' personality and find change to be
difficult at times. Please don't throw any new ideas at me! It
will change my whole schedule!

"One of the first new ideas thrown at me was the *You Are
Smarter Than You Think!* program, which showed me what
I thought I already knew: Yes, I am an auditory *Experiential
Learner*. Bearing in mind that I didn't learn anything new from
this, I continued to study the way I always had. Every day after
school and on the weekends, I reread my notes over and over
for hours. I received a low 80 on my first test and was shocked
to get a 73 on my final. I was upset because I had always been
a B+ or A student. So, what happened?

"History began to repeat itself during the next semester. When
I received a low-80s grade on a test, I realized that I had to do
something. It was obvious that information was not staying in
my long-term memory. I despised taping classes (How can I
remember to bring the tape recorder? Do I have enough tapes
and working batteries? When am I ever going to have time
to listen to this? Is it really going to work?), but I gave in.

"I have now taped several weeks of classes and have listened to the tapes the same night. It takes far less time to listen to the tapes than to reread. I have retained much more information. I feel much more confident participating in discussions with other students—a strategy which also helps to move information to my long-term memory! My next step is to increase my time spent in the Nursing Arts Laboratory to use my experiential learning style!

"If you have the same attitude I had about study habits and not getting anything out of **YASTYT**, I hope that my story will help push you in the right direction. I am a great skeptic and difficult to change, but I found that the program helped me a great deal. Good luck."

You Are Smarter Than You Think! *is a great learning tool.*

-Southern California
Nursing Student

CHANGE IS SCARIER THAN FAILURE

We will use the same technique, test after test, failing the whole way, hoping that by some magical stroke, the technique will suddenly work. Some of us have had great success before this. We are comfortable with our old techniques. Why do we need these new techniques? Can the situation be that different? Change takes courage. Some of us need to know the benefits before we will risk change. Change is risky.

Many of you have been assigned this book because your instructors thought you could benefit from it. Others of you are reading it because your successes have been few and far between. The question is, are you willing to risk change to experience the benefits? Today's world is never static. The winners will be the ones who can meet the need for change with curiosity and an open mind. Remember the list of the benefits that were reported to me by the students that I mentioned earlier? These students were just like you. Many of them had been successful in their under graduate classes, but when learning got more demanding, something new had to kick in. The **YASTYT** learning system provided that support. Some of you have never had much academic success. You don't even know what it feels like. But if you focus on these benefits, they will inspire you and keep you going. Just to refresh your memory here is an expanded version of the list.

Graphics this page courtesy of Totem Graphics, Inc. and Corel Corp.

THE BENEFITS OF USING THIS SYSTEM, ACCORDING TO STUDENTS

1. *You will learn quicker.* Just think of it. You will be able to learn information in one-third less time. That means a 12- hour session is reduced to an 8-hour session. Four extra hours just for you to do with as you wish.

2. *The information will stay with you longer.* No more learning and forgetting. What a waste of your time and effort. With the **YASTYT** method, what you learn will stay with you so that you can use it.

3. *You will be able to think critically.* Is critical thinking difficult for you? It is for many. It's difficult not because you are stupid but because you are trying to use short-term memory to do it. Long-term memory and critical thinking go hand in hand.

4. *Studying for the next test will be easier.* The first time information is stored in long-term memory it creates a path to that information. When new information comes along that can be associated with this old information, it flies into long-term memory almost instantly.

5. *You will have less stress.* When you know that you know, tests are a snap. Wouldn't it feel wonderful not to get so nervous over a test every time one comes up?

6. *You can get better grades.* I know this isn't an issue for some of you. But for those of you who could use some improvement in this area, I think you will be pleased. Most people who use the **YASTYT** Learning System hover around the A grade level even if they were hanging around a much lower category before.

7. *Improved self-esteem.* Ninety-three percent of the students who used the **YASTYT** system over the last five years have reported that they feel better about themselves after using the system. Wouldn't you love to have that feeling?

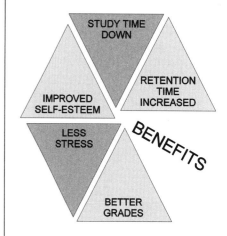

This system helped me to sleep more, study less, feel more secure and get better grades on my tests.

-Michigan
Nursing Student

THE NEXT STEP

I am now going to show you step by step how to use your personal attributes to transform any learning situation into a winning situation.

I realize that learning needs come in many different forms. However, in the next three sections I will show you how to read and learn textbook material using your attributes. Later you can apply this information to your own particular learning needs.

As I mentioned earlier, this book is coded with icons for your convenience. You will not be reading every page from this point on. You will only read the pages that pertain specifically to you and your attributes. It is important that you read this material in sequence. Everyone must also read all pages without icons, which will be referred to as the *white pages*.

THIS IS AN EASY PROCESS

Using the **You** Are Smarter Than You Think*!* learning system is a simple, three-step process.

The three steps are:

- reception

- reorganization

- retention

The following story about a rancher and his sheep will help you to remember these three steps:

Illustration A

There was once a rancher who had a herd of sheep. (*See Illustration A.*) These sheep were all bunched together in a pen. The rancher wanted to get his best sheep to the barn for the winter and his other sheep to market. In order to do this, he knew that he had to first get into his sheep pen. The best way for him to get into the pen was to go through the gate. Since the gate was closed, the easiest action for him to take was just to open the gate, so he did this. (*See Illustration B.*)

Illustration B

The first step in the **You** Are Smarter Than You Think*!* learning system is *Reception*. Many of you think you have been receiving information when listening to a lecture or reading a textbook. How many times have you had to reread a chapter or paragraph because you had no idea what you had just read? The truth is, many times the gate to your brain has been closed. The information that you thought you received never got in. This would not have happened if you had simply opened your *Reception* gate.

Now back to the story about our rancher. In his first action, the rancher got into the pen by opening the gate. Now he must separate the best sheep from the ones that will go to market. He must cut the sheep and reorganize them so that they it be easy to herd them to the barn. (*See Illustration C*)

In the next chapter, I will discuss the second step in the **You** *Are Smarter Than You Think!* learning system. This step is called *Reorganization*. Just as the rancher knew that not all his sheep were good enough to keep, you know that not all of the information that you read in textbooks or hear in lectures is important enough to learn. In addition, textbook and lecture information is often poorly organized. I have found that brains have specific organizational needs and if these needs are violated, learning is more difficult.

How many times have you been confused or overwhelmed by what you were reading? How stupid has it made you feel? Clarity would have come if you had reorganized the information just as the farmer cut and reorganized his sheep.

Our rancher must now move his prized sheep to the barn where they will be safe from wolves and foul weather. (*See Illustration D*) Because he is a smart rancher, he will not herd his sheep over the mountains or across great rivers. He will instead take the path that is flattest and most direct to the barn. (Illustrations courtesy of Jeanne Hallinan.)

In chapter five the third step in the **You** *Are Smarter Than You Think!* learning system will be discussed. This step is called *Retention*.

If you have been using memorizing as a tool for learning, you have been herding your best information over high hills and across enormous rivers. You may have thought that you had gotten these pieces of information to the barn, when in fact, you probably only made it to a short-term shelter (short-term memory). In this short-term shelter, you probably discovered that your information was gobbled up by the wolves of time.

How frustrating has it felt to have studied so hard and realized that 24 hours after the test, all that you learned was gone? The way to the barn and the way to long-term memory is always the shortest route. If you had taken this route using the *Retention* step, your learning would still be in the barn.

If you can remember this story about the rancher and his sheep, you can remember to use the **You** *Are Smarter Than You Think!* learning system. Again the three steps are, *Reception*, *Reorganization*, and *Retention*.

If you will now look on your *Personal Learning Summary* sheet (*Page 17*), you will see the three categories mentioned above: *Reception*, *Reorganization*, and *Retention*. You will also notice that *Auditory*, *Visual*, and Combination *Language Processing* skills refer to *Reception*. The *Linguistic*, *Logical*, and *Spatial*

Illustration C

Illustration D

I was quite nervous about the different style of testing in nursing, but with this system my nerves are no big deal.

-Wisconsin
Nursing Student

*Getting better grades makes me feel good, and the **YASTYT** system did this for me.*

-Wisconsin
Nursing Student

With this system I find that I am doing a lot less reading in the textbook and this makes me feel less stressful.

-Pennsylvania
Nursing Student

skills refer to *Reorganization.* The *Musical, Body Kinesthetic, Knowing Self,* and *Knowing Others* skills refer to *Retention.*

We are now going to take a closer look at *Reception.*

APPLYING YOUR RECEPTION ATTRIBUTE

I want you to understand something very important. The scores you received in the *Reception* area refer to your ability to process language only. Some of you have had other evaluations in the past that have indicated you were Auditory or Visual, and now maybe on this evaluation you found that you were combination. Don't get confused. These two tests were looking at different things. For our purposes here we are looking only at how you process language best, nothing more.

Several years ago, I was working with a student who was also working full time while going to school. When we evaluated his *Reception* abilities, we discovered that he had a two in *Auditory,* a three in *Visual* and a nine in *Combination.* As we were reviewing this information, his eyes got very big and he said, "Now I understand why." He went on to explain that his wife frequently calls him at work and asks him to pick up things at the store on his way home, but he always forgets to do it. He explained that he intends to follow through, but by the time work is finished, he has forgotten. His scores explained the reason. He would hear her request over the phone (*Auditory*); he just didn't remember it. His solution: write down her requests. Whenever he did this, the item was picked up.

THE FIRST STEP

We are first going to look at the *Reception* step because it is so important to the classroom experience. It is important because the way in which you process language is the foundation to most learning. If you can't process or receive what is being said or read, how can you learn it? It just doesn't get in. I know many of you have had the experience of reading something and when you were finished, you knew you had read it but you did not have a clue as to *what* you had read.

Please look at the *Reception* section on your *Personal Learning Summary.* Notice which icon you circled, then find the pages tipped with that icon and read only those pages. These pages will show you how to apply your attributes. For example: Let's say that you circled the *eye* icon. When you finish reading these *white pages* without icons, you will move to the pages tipped with an *eye* and read only those pages. Be sure to read the introductory paragraph for each section. These will always be on the *white pages* preceding the pages with icons. This introductory information will help you have a better understanding of why you are doing what you are doing.

HONOR YOUR STRENGTHS

I want you to know that being stronger in one area over another is perfectly normal. Our Creator wanted us to be different, and this is one way in which we are. It is not better to be stronger in one area than in another. What is important is that you honor your strengths and forget about your weaknesses. If you will honor your strengths, they will honor you.

WHAT ABOUT A TIE?

If you have a tie in two of the categories, read both strategies. You can use both of the ideas given when appropriate. If you have a tie in all three categories, this means you do not have a *Reception* preference. You process language well no matter what modality you *use*. You may move on to the *Reorganization Attribute—How to use it* chapter 4. (*Page 57*)

SCORES FOUR AND BELOW IN ALL CATEGORIES?

I have found over the years that in order to survive high-level learning environments like graduate school, nursing school, and law school, you must process language at a high level. Why? The textbooks and reading material in these arenas are much more complex. The ideas discussed are more abstract. If you did not score higher than a four in all three of the *Reception* categories, this does not mean you are stupid. It just means you are encoding language at a lower level than your capacity. This can be due to many different things, and it can be improved easily.

When students who have this type of score participate in English As A Second Language (ESL) classes for one semester and work on their language-processing abilities, usually their scores will improve enough to go on.

Some of you may have already been through ESL classes. Just because you passed the class does not guarantee that you are processing language at a high enough level for graduate school. This may seem like a step backward; but believe me, it will help you tremendously. For those of you who are not bilingual, the ESL program will still help you. It will improve your language processing ability.

If you will take the time to improve your language processing skills, you will discover how brilliant you truly are. Ignoring this one skill will keep you from accessing that brilliance. Don't let that happen to you. You deserve better.

Now, please turn to the icon-tipped pages corresponding to your highest score.

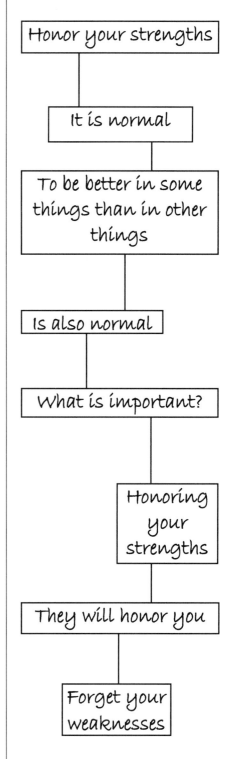

Auditory Language Processor

If you circled the ear icon, it means that you learn best through hearing. This means that whenever you really want to learn something, you need to hear it. *Not* see it, but *hear* it. It means that it is your responsibility to transform any learning situation into a listening situation.

DURING LECTURES

During a lecture, you would be better off just listening to it and either taping it or getting notes from someone else for later use. Some of your instructors will not allow you to record in class; however, many are more than willing to change their rules when they realize why you want to tape them.

A student once told me this story. One of her instructors told her students adamantly that no one was to tape her class. So the student went to the instructor's office, and in a very nice way explained why she would like permission to use a tape recorder. After hearing this explanation, the instructor was more than happy to accommodate this girl. Moral: understanding opens many closed doors.

If you are not able to tape a class, don't let this stop you. Get the notes from someone else just listen to the lecture. You will learn far more by listening and getting your notes later. Be sure to choose a good note taker.

TEXTBOOK READING

As an *Auditory Language Processor* you need to hear your textbook instead of reading it. There are two ways to do this. One is to get a tape of your textbook from the disabled student center on your campus; the other is team up with a *Combination Language Processor* who has to read the textbook aloud. As the text is being read you may want to tape it so that you can listen to it later.

STUDYING

Always study aloud. Talk to yourself or listen to a tape player.

Reading my notes out loud into a tape recorder made me remember the information. I would play the tape back and read my notes again, which made me concentrate on the information. I think this book is an asset for anyone.

-Pennsylvania
Nursing Student

This is a great program for people who need to save time.

-Pennsylvania
Nursing Student

TEST TAKING

During a test, you should read questions very carefully, trying to hear the words in your head. Say the word cat silently to yourself right now. Can you hear it in your head? That is what I mean. But only do this during a test when no other option is available.

Remember, as an *Auditory Language Processor*, whenever you really want to learn something, you should hear it. A tape recorder and a reading partner are your best friends. Start using them. Honor your strengths and they will honor you.

Now turn to the next set of *white pages* (*Page 57*) unless you had a tie and need to read about an additional strategy.

Visual Language Processor

If you circled the eye icon, you are *Visually* talented. This means that you learn information best if you can read it. *Not* by hearing it, but by *reading* it. It is your responsibility to transform any learning situation into a situation where you can read.

DURING LECTURES
In lectures, it is important that you focus on any visual aides that are being used. Write key words down, and I recommend you double-check your notes with someone else who is a good note taker. You may miss a considerable amount of the information when listening to a lecture while taking notes, because this is a *Combination Language Processing* skill. If you have a high score in combination also, then it should not be as difficult for you. My *Visual Language Processing* students have always found that double-checking their notes with someone or with a tape recorder after class really helps.

TEXTBOOK READING
When reading a textbook, you should read silently.

STUDYING
When you want to definitely learn something, you should read and study the material visually.

TEST TAKING
During a test, you should do the same, read silently. Honor your strengths and they will honor you.

Now turn to the next set of *white pages* (*Page 57*), unless you had a tie and need to read about an additional strategy.

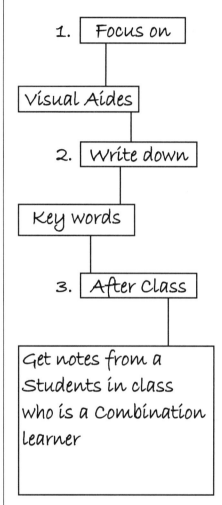

Combination Language Processor

If you circled the eye/ear icon, you are a *Combination Language Processor.* This means that you learn best when information is both heard and read together. It is your responsibility to transform any learning situation into a combination situation.

DURING LECTURES

Note taking is a combination skill. You need to become a very good note taker so that you can maximize learning during a lecture situation. A four-in-one color pen can help you differentiate between main and subpoints. Learning to use this pen will help you organize your note taking.

If note taking is difficult for you, adapt the *Reorganization* skill that you will learn next. I think with a little practice you will find these techniques very helpful.

TEXTBOOK READING

When reading a textbook, read aloud. (Be a friend to your *Auditory Language Processor* friends and read to them. They need you.) This means that from now on, except when reading for pleasure, you must have words coming out of your mouth when you read and study.

STUDYING

When studying, you must again read and study aloud. No more silent studying for you. Honor your strengths and they will honor you.

TEST TAKING

On tests, you must learn to speak very softly—subvocalize. This can make a tremendous impact on your final performance. Many of my students have learned how to do this with great success. They do not disturb other classmates because the vocal is so soft. Some students have also found that they can simply read and hear the words in their head without sub-vocalizing.

Now turn to the next set of *white pages* (*Page 57*), unless you had a tie and need to read about an additional strategy.

1. *Note taking is a combination skill,*

2. *You need to become a great note taker.*

3. *Use a 4 in one pen. It will help categorize your main and sub points.*

This learning system has given me permission to utilize my own learning techniques.

Growing up in a parochial school, I was taught to 'follow with my eyes and to read silently.

> -Pennsylvania Nursing Student

Reorganization attribute
How to use it

He that will not apply new remedies must expect new evils.

—Bacon

Chapter

4

In this chapter you will learn about the second step in the **YASTYT** *Learning System. Here you will begin to understand why textbook material has been so time consuming or difficult for you. I think you will find the activities in this chapter helpful.*

Now that you know how to effectively receive the information you want to learn, you are ready for the next step. You are ready to learn how to use your *Reorganization Attribute*.

What in the world do I mean by Reorganization and what does this have to do with improving your learning? Your brain has its own specialized organizational needs. If information gets into the brain through the correct reception channel but is organized contrary to its needs, your brain will have difficulties remembering this information.

Most information that we want to learn is not handed to us on a silver platter. We must extract it out of books, articles, and sometimes even lectures. If we extract this information in an organizational structure which suits our brain, much of what we extract we will learn easily.

MOST LEARNING ENCOMPASSES WRITTEN MATERIAL

I estimate that only about one-third of our population deals effectively with written material. The rest of us are overwhelmed by it, and it has a tendency to put us to sleep. We read this material several times in the hopes of learning something. Sometimes we will highlight important phrases, and before we know it, the pages have magically gone from white to hot pink because everything we read seems important. I am here to tell those of you who can relate to this that your days of frustration are numbered.

Illustration E

This program really did help when I used it.

-Pennsylvania
Nursing Student

With this system I can study in a shorter period of time and retain more information.

-Pennsylvania
Nursing Student

LET'S FIND OUT WHAT YOUR BRAIN NEEDS

Look at your *Personal Learning Summary* and look under the *Reorganization* section. You should see an icon, which you circled. That icon is an indication of what organizational style your brain needs. The *Reorganization* process you are about to learn will allow you to read material one time through, and in the process, learn a great deal of the material. I am talking here about making every step count. Many of you have wasted too much time rereading material you weren't comprehending and certainly weren't learning. From this day forward, you should never reread anything. Make the first time count.

IF YOUR STRATEGY DOESN'T FEEL RIGHT

A few of you may feel that the strategy you will read below just doesn't work for you. I suggest that you give it a little time to work and if it continues to feel difficult and not very helpful, try another strategy or modify it. The ideas that will be given to you are merely suggestions. If an idea does not feel exactly correct, modify it to your liking. This is about you discovering what works for you. The learning style inventory for discovering your attributes is not always perfect, so it might be necessary to just play around with several of the strategies and discover the one that works best for you.

YOU WILL BE DOING WHAT WORKS FOR YOU

Each of you will be learning your own specialized way of reorganizing based on your brain's needs.

Look again at your *Personal Learning Summary*. Look under the section titled *Reorganization*. What icon did you circle? Please read the pages tipped with this icon now and learn how to Reorganize. If you have a tie, please read on. Otherwise, move directly to the first page of your *Reorganization* section.

IF YOU HAD A TIE

Some of you may have had a tie in two of the above *Reorganization* categories. One of these areas may feel stronger than the other, and the strategy listed below may feel perfect for you. If not, try combining two of the strategies. Don't make this difficult. Just take some of the ideas from one strategy and blend it with another one. Here are some examples:

Reorganization Tie Chart

YOUR STYLE	Lecture	Textbook	Test Study	Test Taking
LINGUISTIC/ SPATIAL	Focus on the words. Take Simple notes using Maps and Color	Words are King. Use the correct ones for you. Put important information on separate pieces of a paper using Maps and Color.	Review your Maps. Add your Reception and Retention components.	N/A -you will use other skills here
LINGUISTIC/ LOGICAL	Focus on the words and use outlines to organize important material.	Words are king. Focus on using words that make sense to you and organize important information in outlines on separate pieces of paper.	Review your outlines adding your Reception and Retention components.	N/A - You will use other skills here.
SPATIAL/LOGICAL	Simplify and organize what is being talked about in a sequential format.	Use the Logical system, outlines but simplify everything using outlines and color.	Review your map or outlines adding your Reception and Retention components.	N/A – You will use other skills here.

Now, read in detail the strategies for each of your abilities. When you are finished, I think you will have a better understanding of what I have been talking about and will easily see a solution for yourself. Don't make this hard. A tie means you just have more to work with and that is good. Now, you may move on to the icon pages that correspond to your attributes.

Linguistic

If you circled the mouth icon, you are a person who needs and loves words. Words, *not* pictures, help you to understand. The more words the better. Word accuracy is also crucial.

The sky isn't just blue to you. The sky is crimson blue, dotted with cottony white clouds laced with yellow.

ACTIVITY ★

Look at the photograph below. Take five minutes and talk to yourself about what you see. Be very specific. Explore with your words. Let them tell you what you see. Ask yourself questions like the following and then answer them. Why do you think the boys are being carried like this? What is the boy on the left thinking? Who is carrying them? How old are these kids? Talk about their hair. Keep asking yourself questions like this.

Photograph courtesy of Christopher Briscoe, Ashland, OR.

- Did you feel a little uncomfortable when you first had to look at this picture and there were no words?

- How did your words help you to see this picture more completely?

- What did your words show you that your eyes might have missed?

Most textbooks are written by *Linguistically* talented people. This is good for you. You feel comfortable reading their work. The problem comes when you want to glean from the material that which is most important. Because you love words, everything seems important. In the past, I have allowed my

Words are King!

This learning system has made me feel more confident.

> -Ohio
> Nursing Student

Retaining more for longer periods of time helps me to feel competent. This is just one of the benefits of the **YASTYT** *system.*

> -So. California
> Nursing Student

Linguistic Learners to highlight. I quickly learned that when students use this technique, everything turns hot pink because everything seems important. I have stopped making this suggestion.

As you experienced above, your exact and specific words helped you to understand the picture. It is not good enough for you to know that the boy went to the store. You also need to know why, when, and what the boy looked like. All these details help you to more fully understand the main point.

When you reorganize textbook material, you will be allowed to highlight only the main points. You will then be asked to write about these main points in your own words because your words will have more meaning than the book's. Here are the steps you will take.

THE LINGUISTIC REORGANIZATION STEPS

There are four steps in the *Linguistic Reorganization* process. Simply put, this is what you do when reading a textbook:

1. *Remember* to use your *Auditory*, *Visual*, or *Combination Language Processing* skill;

2. *Survey* the chapter;

3. *Use* the *Modified Highlighting* step to read the chapter;

4. *Scan* the chapter summary and/or study guide. Let's take a look at each of these steps in detail.

The First Step

Remember to use your best *Reception* channel. Are you *Auditory*, *Visual*, or *Combination*? Your answer to this question will determine the most effective way for you to read. If you are not sure about your *Reception* channel, refer to the *Reception* chapter on *Page 43*.

The Second Step

Next, *Survey* the chapter you are going to read. If you do this surveying process correctly, it should take you only five minutes per chapter. These five minutes will save you time in the long run. This process prepares your brain to receive information and gets you interested in the subject. It gets your curiosity going. Remember, we only learn what we want to learn.

Surveying the chapter means reading over all major headings. Major chapter headings are the major boldfaced headings that appear throughout a chapter. Most chapters have six or seven of these. If you will look at our example on the facing page, you will see that there is a title, plus major, and minor headings. Usually, the minor headings are in smaller or less bold print.

This book gave a big boost to my self-esteem, which I was needing because nursing is so difficult.

-Pennsylvania
Nursing Student

My grades are just as good, but with this system, I don't need to spend as much time studying.

-Pennsylvania
Nursing Student

WHAT IS PSYCHOLOGY?

Psychology, like other sciences, seeks to describe, explain, predict, and control the events it studies.

WHAT DO PSYCHOLOGISTS DO?

Psychologists share a keen interest in behavior, but in other ways they may differ markedly.

Clinical Counseling Psychologists

Clinical psychologists specialize in helping people with psychological problems adjust to the demands of life.

School and Educational Psychologists

School psychologists are employed by school systems to help identify and assist students who encounter problems that interfere with learning.

Developmental Psychologists

Developmental psychologists study the changes—physical, emotional, cognitive, and social—that occur throughout the life span.

FAMOUS PSYCHOLOGISTS

Wilhelm Wundt

Wundt claimed that the mind was a natural event and could be studied scientifically, just like sight, hearing, and the flow of blood. He used the method of introspection, recommended by Socrates, to try to discover the basic element of experience.

William James

The brother of Henry James, William adopted a broader view of psychology that focused on the relation between conscious experience and behavior. James was a major figure in the development of psychology in the United States. He received an MD degree from Harvard University but never practiced medicine.

Major Headings

Minor Headings

Major Heading

Minor Headings

I can honestly say a lot of added stress has been alleviated by using this system.

-New Jersey
Nursing Student

I have passed every exam. I usually don't pass first exams because I don't know what is expected. Now I learn the right things.

-Ohio
Nursing Student

As you identify the major headings, read them one at a time. Then ask yourself two quick questions about each heading, which you will not answer. Why won't you answer them? Because your answer is not important. Getting your mind to come up with the question is what is important, because it will stimulate your curiosity.

Look at the example on *Page 63.* The first major heading is What is Psychology? Read this and then ask yourself a Personal and a *Nonpersonal Question.* A *Personal Question* has something to do with you. *My Personal Question* for this example might be: "I wonder how this word came into existence?" Now come up with your own *Personal Question.* Do it.

Your second question will be a *Nonpersonal Question,* meaning you come up with something not personal to yourself. My *Nonpersonal Question* might be: "I wonder how this word came into existence?" Now it's your turn to make up your *Nonpersonal Question.* Once you have asked your two questions, you are ready to begin the *Modified Highlighting* process.

The Third Step

This step is called *Modified Highlighting.* With this process, you are only going to highlight in a limited way.

It is recommended that you use either a red pen or hot pink highlighter because this will stimulate your visual cortex and help you to remember more easily. (The four-in-one pens are nice to use. They have red and three other colors, which you can use to help isolate different kinds of information.)

On a given page of reading, such as in a textbook, you are allowed to highlight only the main points. This will probably be only one or two sentences per page. Next, you are to read the support material under these main points. Last, in the margins or on a separate piece of paper, rewrite this support information, using your own words. The simple act of putting ideas in your own words will help you to more fully understand the main points you have highlighted.

The support material should be written so that it expands your understanding of the main points. Pay close attention to the words you use. Be careful not to change the meaning of the main point. Remember, words form your brain's organizational structure and are crucial to your understanding and learning process.

An Example

On the next two pages, you will see exactly how this modified highlighting step is done. This example is taken from the book, *Men Are From Mars and Women Are From Venus*, by John Gray, Ph.D. Review it carefully so that you will be able to duplicate this process with your own reading. You will notice that what I wrote in the margin notes is probably not what you would write. Each of you needs to find your own words that will help you to more fully understand the main points.

I feel better prepared and more in control with this system.

-Pennsylvania
Nursing Student

I still remember material I learned four months ago with this system!

-Pennsylvania
Nursing Student

Men Are From Mars and Women Are From Venus

Copyright © 1992 by John Gray

Reprinted by permission of Harper Collins Publishers, Inc.

LINGUISTIC REORGANIZATION EXAMPLE

Margin Notes	Book Text

LIFE ON MARS

Martians value power, competency, efficiency, and achievement.

They are the power brokers. They thrive on power and skill and proving themselves. Their sense of self comes from their results.

They are always doing things to prove themselves and develop their power and skills. Their sense of self is defined through their ability to achieve results. They experience fulfillment primarily through success and accomplishment.

Like Dad, they primarily experience fulfillment through success and accomplishment.

Everything on Mars is a refection of these values.

They don't just dress for success but dress to express. Dress gives power to their jobs and to their egos.

Even their dress is designed to reflect their skills and competence. Police officers, soldiers, businessmen, scientists, cab drivers, technicians, and chefs all wear uniforms or at least hats to reflect their competence and power.

You would never catch them reading a "touchy-feely" magazine like *Psychology Today* or romance novels or self-help books—they do not need help. They need results.

They don't read magazines like *Psychology Today, Self*, or *People*. They are more concerned with outdoor activities like hunting, fishing, and racing cars. They are interested in the news, weather, and sports and couldn't care less about romance novels and self- help books.

They are the jocks, the sports buffs. Just give them the weather and news and they are happy.

They are more interested in *objects* and *things* rather than people and feelings. Even today on Earth, while women fantasize about romance, men fantasize about powerful cars, faster computers, gadgets, gizmos, and new more powerful technology. Men are preoccupied with the *things* that can help them express power by creating results and achieving their goals.

They are not romantic. They do not fantasize about romance. They only want objects and things—faster cars, computers, tools—things! Anything that will help them reach their goals and produce results.

LINGUISTIC REORGANIZATION EXAMPLE

Book Text	Margin Notes
LIFE ON VENUS Venusians have different values. They value love, communication, beauty, and relationships. They spend a lot of time supporting, helping, and nurturing one another. Their sense of self is defined through their feelings and the quality of their relationships. They experience fulfillment through sharing and relating. Everything on Venus reflects these values. Rather than building highways and tall buildings, the Venusians are more concerned with living together in harmony, community, and loving cooperation. Relationships are more important than work and technology. In most ways their world is the opposite of Mars. They do not wear uniforms like the Martians (to reveal their competence). On the contrary, they enjoy wearing a different outfit every day, according to how they are feeling. Personal expression, especially of their feelings, is very important. They may even change outfits several times a day as their mood changes. Communication is of primary importance. To share their personal feelings is much more important than achieving goals and success. Talking and relating to one another are a source of tremendous fulfillment.	Venusians are *people* people. Like my mother, they love to talk with their friends and help them with their problems. Goals are not as important as the status of their relationships. They experience satisfaction through sharing and relating. The Venusian world does not have super highways, buildings, and external accomplishments. Their life reflects living together in harmonious relationships. Their clothing is an expression of who they are, not what they do. They may change their outfits several times during the day as their moods change. Going to lunch and sharing with their friends is more important than achieving a goal. It is their source of fulfillment.

Men Are From Mars and Women Are From Venus
Copyright © 1992 by John Gray
Reprinted by permission of Harper Collins Publishers, Inc.

You may have noticed that I made references to my parents earlier on. They were very much like Martians and Venusians. My memories of them helped me to more fully understand the specifics of each personality type. Remember to do the same. Personalize wherever you can.

The Fourth Step

Once you have finished the survey and the *Modified Highlighting* steps, you are ready for the final and last step of our extraction process. This step, *Scan*, involves fast reading of the study guide or chapter summary.

Many of my students tell me that they study the wrong things for tests. The *Survey* and *Modified Highlighting* steps should help you with this. It is also helpful to quickly read over the chapter summary or study guide to make sure that you included all the important information. Chapter summaries are usually found at the back of each chapter, but sometimes they are at the beginning of a chapter. Study guides are usually available through your instructor, and sometimes your bookstore will have them for the more popular classes.

If you read something in the chapter summary or study guide that doesn't sound familiar, you should immediately go back to the chapter, find the original reference, and include that in your *Modified Highlighting*. When you find that you are studying the correct material for tests, you may drop this step.

THE LINGUISTIC MEMORY JOGGER

This completes the *Linguistic Reorganization* process. You are now ready to learn about the *Retention* step. Before you do this, turn to the next page. There you will find your *Memory Jogger*.

This sheet is designed to jog your memory. If you forget a step while you are studying, you can refer to this sheet. This system is simple, and it is easy to drop a step. The *Memory Jogger* is a tool you can use constantly to keep yourself on track. Tear it out and use it!

If you need help on a particular step, go to the page numbers listed on your *Memory Jogger* for the information you need.

For now, fill in the date, your name, and circle your *Reception Attribute*. You will receive further instructions on how to fill out the rest of the form later.

When you have finished this, you may move on to *Page 101* (the *white pages* at the beginning of the *Retention attribute— How to use it* chapter).

This learning system has helped me to become better organized.

-Ohio
Nursing Student

*I am now in control as a result of using the **YASTYT** system.*

-New York State
Nursing Student

LINGUISTIC MEMORY JOGGER

Date: _____

I am a Linguistic Learner   _____
                                                        name

RECEPTION   (*see page 43*)

I am (circle which you are) Auditory, Visual or Combination Language Processor.

REORGANIZATION   (*see page 57*)

    Your Steps:

    1. Open *Reception Channel*. Use your best.

    2. *Survey* the chapter quickly asking yourself the two questions.

    3. Use *Modified Highlighting*.

    4. *Scan* quickly the chapter summary or study guide.

RETENTION   (*see page 101*)

Instructions will be given later for this section.

    1. If I am a Musical Learner, I need to use music and rhythm when I am learning.
    2. If I am a Body Kinesthetic Learner, I need to do something physical when I learn.
    3. If I am talented in Knowing Self, I need to teach what I am learning to someone or something in order to experience what I am learning.
    4. If I am talented in Knowing Others, I need to transform what I am learning into something concrete and real so that I can experience it.

MY PLAN:
1. During lecture I will:

2. When reading a textbook I will:

3. When studying for a test I will:

4. While taking a test I will:

Logical

If you circled the head icon, you are a *Logical Learner*. *Logical Learners* flourish in a sequentially organized environment.

They are often confused by information that is not well organized. I used to believe that all *Logical Learners* liked the same kind of sequential organization (outlines). What I discovered is that they don't at all.

Logical Learners believe that there is really only one right way to do something, and they feel their way is best.

They have their own specific organizational needs. You will want to discover the kind of organizational system that works best for you.

HERE ARE SOME OPTIONS

You might consider outlines, lists, boxes, individual pages, or 3x5 index cards. One of my students used old calendars and filled in the boxes to organize the material she was going to learn. I recommend to some students that they designate separate sheets of paper for different kinds of information.

In addition, the most important activity you can do for yourself is to make sure that before a test, you know concretely the four or five specific areas you are going to be tested on. If you don't know this, you probably will not do well.

TO DO ★

Look at the list of names below. Can you make much sense of this list in its disorganized state? It is obviously a list of different kinds of sports but what kinds? What do they have in common? How are they different? Not until you organize this list will you fully understand it.

football	baseball	chess
volleyball	sailing	solitaire
badminton	running	ice hockey
croquet	basketball	water-skiing
dominos	biking	skiing
tennis	soccer	golf

On a scrap of paper, organize this list according to the following categories:

- Team sports/Games
- Non-team sports/Games
- Solitary sports/Games

---

1. It is important

2. To make

3. Sequential Lists

I always felt that books were very unorganized. Now I understand how to overcome this problem. I use colored pens when making notes and verbalize when I read. All this makes studying easier and less time consuming.

-Michigan
Nursing Student

It has been more interesting utilizing a systematic approach to studying. I feel more organized which seems to decrease anxiety. I am also studying less hours.

-Pennsylvania
Nursing Student

Outlining has helped me to stay interested. The colors keep me from getting bored.

-Southern CA
Nursing Student

Use your own organizational style to do this activity. Don't let your Logical mind make this difficult. (Use lists, outlines, boxes or whatever you want.)

Look at your organized lists now. What is the one big difference between the sports/games that use balls and the ones that don't? Isn't that interesting?

How did the organizing help you answer this question?

If you did this activity, you should now have an experience of how important organization is to your brain.

TEXTBOOKS ARE NOT FOR YOU

Textbooks are written by Linguistic Learners and their writing is very confusing to your Logical mind. The following example, taken from a textbook, will show you why reading a textbook can be so confusing. For our purposes here, What is Psychology is a major heading. Logical Learners assume that this heading defines what will be talked about in this section. They also assume that the information will be sequentially presented. As you will see in the example, these are incorrect assumptions.

EXAMPLE:

My Comments

This first paragraph is really just background filler, which helps the linguistically talented person but confuses the Logical person.

The first two sentences in the third paragraph answer the question, *What is Psychology?* which is what this section is supposed to be about.

The sentence that begins, "Human behavior..." has nothing to do with what psychology is, and yet it is in the section titled *What is Psychology* and this confuses the *Logical Learner*. If the *Logical Learner* were writing this chapter, this filler information would not be here.

Book Text

What is Psychology?

People love to watch people. Human beings are fascinated by human behavior. We surprise ourselves sometimes with just how interested we are.

Psychologists are also intrigued by the mysteries of behavior and make an effort to answer questions such as why and how. But while most people try to satisfy their curiosity about behavior through casual observations, psychologists focus exclusively on studying human behavior.

Psychology is a scientific approach to the study of behavior. As a science it brings carefully controlled methods of observation, such as the survey and the experiment, to bear on its subject whenever possible.

Human behavior is the biggest interest of most psychologists; however, many of them focus much or all of their research on the behavior of animals, ranging from rats and pigeons to flatworms and gorillas.

Textbooks use charts and graphs which, if they are not *Spatial*, also confuse the *Logical Learner*.

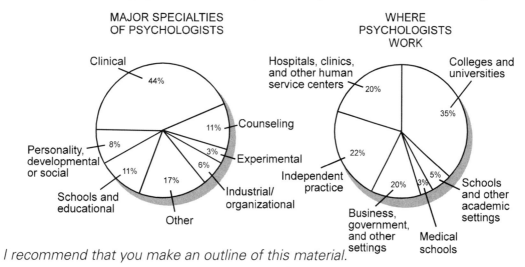

MAJOR SPECIALTIES
OF PSYCHOLOGISTS

WHERE
PSYCHOLOGISTS
WORK

I recommend that you make an outline of this material.

EXAMPLE:

    I. What Do Psychologists Do?

        A. Major specialties of psychologists

            1. 44%-Clinical

            2. 11%-Counseling

            3. 3%-Experimental

            4. 6%-Industrial/organizational

            5. 8%-Personality, developmental, social

            6. 11 %-School/educational

            7. 17%-Other

LOGICAL REORGANIZATION

You are now ready to learn the specifics of the *Logical Reorganization* step. This step asks you to *Pull Out* and put into sequence the important information you want to learn. The key is to make sure the information is sequential. We recommend that you use colored pens or pencils to assist with this reorganization. (The four-colors-in-one pen is very useful.) Colors, especially red, stimulate the visual cortex, and help memory.

Here are the steps you will take:

    1. *Remember* to use your best *Reception* skill (*Auditory, Visual, Combination*);

    2. *Survey* the chapter;

    3. *Pull Out* and put into sequence the important ideas;

    4. *Scan* the chapter summary and/or study guide.

Let's take a look at each of these steps in detail.

*I think the **YASTYT** Learning System enables the students to better utilize their own resources and provides a quick way to organize confusing material.*

        -Pennsylvania
        Nursing Student

I don't go into tests with butterflies in my stomach anymore.

-Pennsylvania
Nursing Student

THE FIRST STEP

Always use your best *Reception* channel. With this system you will be reading textbook material only one time, so make it count.

THE SECOND STEP

Next, in the *Logical Reorganization* process, *Survey* the chapter. This surveying process, if you do it correctly, should take you only five minutes per chapter. These five minutes will save you time in the long run because they prepare your brain to receive information and get you interested in the subject. Curiosity is the key. We only learn what we want to learn.

Survey the chapter by reading the major chapter headings and asking yourself two quick questions which you do not answer. You will not answer the questions, because the answers are not important. The questions open your mind and get it into a receptive mode, and that is what is important.

Major chapter headings are the boldfaced headings that appear throughout a chapter. Most chapters have six or seven of these.

Here's How

If you will look at the example on the next page, you will see that there are a title, and major and minor headings. Usually the minor headings are in smaller print or in less bold print.

As you identify the major headings, read one heading at a time and then ask yourself two quick questions about that heading. Remember, do not answer them.

Look at the example on the next page. The first major heading is What is Psychology? Read this, then ask yourself a *Personal* and a *Nonpersonal Question.*

A *Personal Question* has something to do with you personally. My personal question might be: "I wonder how this word came into existence?" Now, you come up with your personal question.

The second question has to be a *Nonpersonal Question*, which means you come up with something not directly relating to yourself —something that is not personal. My *Nonpersonal Question* might be: "I wonder what kind of people are psychologists?" Now, you make one up.

Color Keeps You Organized

Once you have asked your two quick questions, then write with a colored pen the major heading at the top of a blank sheet of paper. The pen color you choose will be your main point color. You will use this color only for your main points.

This process of putting the major headings on separate pieces of paper is the beginning of reorganizing the important material.

WHAT IS PSYCHOLOGY? ← — — — — — ⎧ *Major Headings*

Psychology, like other sciences, seeks to describe,
explain,predict, and control the events it studies.

WHAT DO PSYCHOLOGISTS DO? ←

Psychologists share a keen interest in behavior, but in other
ways they may differ markedly.

Clinical Counseling Psychologists ←

Clincial psychologists specialize in helping people with
psychological problems adjust to the demands of life.

School and Educational Psychologists ←

School psychologists are employed by school systems to help
identify and assist students who encounter problems that
interfere with learning.

⎧ *Minor Headings*

Developmental Psychologists ←

Developmental psychologists study the changes—physical,
emotional, cognitve, and social—that occur throughout
the life span.

FAMOUS PSYCHOLOGISTS ← — — — — — ⎧ *Major Heading*

Wilhelm Wundt ← — — — —

Wundt claimed that the mind was a natural event and could — — —
be studied scienticially, just like sight, hearing, and the flow of   ⎧ *Minor Headings*
blood. He used the method of introspection, recommended by
Socrates, to try to discover the basic element of experience.

William James ←

The brother of Henry James, William adopted a broader view
of psychhology that focused on the relation between conscious
experience and behavior. James was a major figure in the
development of psychology in the United States. He recieved
an MD degree from Harvard University but never practiced
medicine.

My grade went from a low C to a high B and I am studying less and remembering longer.

-Pennsylvania
Nursing student

I. What is Psychology?

II. What Do Psychologists Do?

III. Famous Psychologists

Figure 7

When you are finished with the survey step, you will have seven or eight sheets of paper with a single heading at the top of each page. The number of pages will be determined by the number of major headings in the chapter.

If you will turn to the next page, you can see what one page should look like. Notice I have placed a roman numeral in front of the heading. The organizational style that I will be using for this demonstration is outline, thus the Roman numerals. You may use whatever style you wish.

For an outline format, the first major heading on the first page will have a Roman numeral I. On the next page, the second heading will have a Roman numeral II, and so on.

THE THIRD STEP

The third step in the *Logical Reorganization* process is to *Pull Out* and put into sequence important information. You have already begun this reorganizing process with the listing of the major headings on separate pieces of paper.

The color that you used for these headings is your main point color. These headings become your main points and determine what information you will *Pull Out* and sequentialize.

The main points or major headings will guide you to what is important. As you read, you will want to find the subpoints and the sub-subpoints that relate to the main points and then record this information under the appropriate headings.

You will be working with three colored pens while doing this process. As I stated earlier, I recommend the pen that has four colors, but you can use three separate pens if you choose.

Let's say, for example, that we wrote our main point in red.

All of your subpoints will be written in a second color, such as green. Your sub-subpoints will be written in a third color, such as blue. These colors will help your mind see a distinction between the main, sub and sub-subpoints and this will help your mind comprehend and remember easier.

EXAMPLE:

Let's say that you have listed on three separate pieces of paper the following headings in red ink:

- What Is Psychology?

- What Do Psychologists do?

- Famous Psychologists

I. What Is Psychology?   (Write in your main-point color.)

I. What is Psychology?   (red)

   A. Psychology Is the Study of
   Human Behavior   (green)

II. What Do Psychologists Do?   (red)

   A. Psychologists Study this
   Behavior Using Experiments and
   Through Observation.   (green)

III. Famous Psychologists   (red)

   A. Freud Is Known as the
   Father of Psychology.   (green)

Figure 8

Outlining Questions?

♦   Essentially, a main point
is a general statement about
some subject such as, What
is Psychology?

♦   A sub-point tells you
more about the main point.

♦   A sub-subpoint tells you
more about the sub-point.

EXAMPLE:

OUTLINE FORM

I. Main point

   A. Sub-point

      1. Sub-sub point

Figure 9

In a textbook you read:

> "Psychology is the study of human behavior.
> Psychologists study this behavior, using
> experiments and through observation. Freud is
> known as the Father of Psychology."

With this *Pull Out* and put into sequence step, you will
pull out and outline the important information under the
appropriate heading. (*See Figure 8*.) Information that talks
about *What is Psychology* goes on the page with the heading
What is Psychology. Information that talks about *What
Psychologists Do* goes on the page with that heading, and so
on. When you finish this step, you will have five or six pages
with the chapter's most important information completely
sequentialized.

THE FOURTH STEP

The last step in the *Logical Reorganization* process is to *Scan*
the chapter summary and/or study guide.

Many of my students have told me that they seem to study the
wrong material for tests. By scanning the chapter summary or
study guide, you can eliminate this problem.

Chapter summaries are usually found at the end of each
chapter, but sometimes they are at the beginning of a chapter.
Study guides are usually available through your instructor.
Bookstores often will have them for the more popular classes.

While scanning, if you discover some material that you did not
write down during the *Pull Out* step, do so at that time.

Material that appears in chapter summaries and study guides is
often also on tests.

You should do this step quickly. Do not spend a great deal of
time. When you find that you are studying the correct material
for tests, you may drop this step.

The following example shows you how your papers should look
after doing the *Logical Reorganization* process. Look it over
carefully so that you can duplicate this process with your own
reading. Don't be too concerned if you would have outlined
this information differently. This is not an exact science. The
selection is taken from *Men Are From Mars and Women Are
From Venus*, by John Gray, Ph.D.

LOGICAL REORGANIZATION EXAMPLE

Book Text	Logical Reorganized Final Product

LIFE ON MARS
 	
Martians value power, competency, efficiency, and achievement. They are always doing things to prove themselves and develop their power and skills. Their sense of self is defined through their ability to achieve results. They experience fulfillment primarily through success and accomplishment.
 	
Everything on Mars is a refection of these values. Even their dress is designed to reflect their skills and competence. Police officers, soldiers, businessmen, scientists, cab drivers, technicians, and chefs all wear uniforms or at least hats to reflect their competence and power.
 	
They don't read magazines like *Psychology Today*, *Self*, or *People*. They are more concerned with outdoor activities like hunting, fishing, and racing cars. They are interested in the news, weather, and sports and couldn't care less about romance novels and self-help books. They are more interested in *objects* and *things* rather than people and feelings. Even today on earth, while women fantasize about romance, men fantasize about powerful cars, faster computers, gadgets, gizmos, and new more powerful technology. Men are preoccupied with the *things* that can help them express power by creating results and achieving their goals.
	I. LIFE ON MARS (red)
	
	  A. Martians value power, competency, efficiency and achievement. (green)
	
	    1. They are always doing things to prove themselves. (blue)
	
	    2. Their results define their sense of self. Self- fulfillment is experienced through success and accomplishment.
	
	  B. Everything on Mars is a reflection of these values.
	
	    1. Dress/uniforms reflect their skills and competence.
	
	    2. They don't read magazines like *Psychology Today*, *Self*, or *People*.
	
	    3. Martians love hunting, fishing, racing cars, news, weather, and sports.
	
	  C. They are more interested in *objects* and *things* rather than people and feelings.
	
	    1. They like things that help them express power by creating results and achieving their goals.
	
	    2. They love new gadgets and faster cars.
	
	    3. They do not like romance novels and self-help books.

Men Are From Mars and Women Are From Venus
Copyright © 1992 by John Gray
Reprinted by permission of HarperCollinsPublishers, Inc.

LOGICAL REORGANIZATION EXAMPLE

Logical Reorganized Final Product	**Book Text**

II. LIFE ON VENUS (red)
 	
  A. Venusians value love, communication, beauty and relationships. (green)
 	
    1. They spend time supporting, helping and nurturing. (blue)
 	
    2. Their sense of self is defined through their feelings and the quality of their relationships.
 	
  B. Everything on Venus reflects these values.
 	
    1. They are concerned with living together in harmony, community, and loving cooperation.
 	
    2. Relationships are more important than work and technology.
 	
  C. They do not wear uniforms.
 	
    1. Expression of their personal feelings is very important.
 	
    2. They wear clothing that reflects their daily feelings.
 	
  D. Communication is of primary importance.
 	
    1. Sharing feelings is more important than achievement.
 	
    2. Fulfillment comes from this sharing.
	LIFE ON MARS
	
	Venusians have different values. They value love, communication, beauty, and relationships. They spend a lot of time supporting, helping, and nurturing one another. Their sense of self is defined through their feelings and the quality of their relationships. They experience fulfillment through sharing and relating.
	
	Everything on Venus reflects these values. Rather than building highways and tall buildings, the Venusians are more concerned with living together in harmony, community, and loving cooperation. Relationships are more important than work and technology. In most ways their world is the opposite of Mars.
	
	They do not wear uniforms like the Martians (to reveal their competence). On the contrary, they enjoy wearing a different outfit every day, according to how they are feeling. Personal expression, especially of their feelings, is very important. They may even change outfits several times a day as their mood changes.
	
	Communication is of primary importance. To share their personal feeling is much more important than achieving goals and success. Talking and relating to one another are a source of tremendous fulfillment.
	
	Men Are From Mars and Women Are From Venus
	Copyright © 1992 by John Gray
	Reprinted by permission of HarperCollinsPublishers, Inc.

THE LOGICAL MEMORY JOGGER

This completes the *Logical Reorganization* process. You are now ready to learn about the *Retention* step. Before you turn to these pages, please turn to next page. There you will find your *Memory Jogger*.

This sheet is designed to jog your memory. If you forget a step while you are studying, you can refer to this sheet. This system is simple, and it is easy to drop a step. The *Memory Jogger* is a tool you can use constantly to keep yourself on track. Tear it out and use it!

If you need help on a particular step, go to the page numbers listed on your *Memory Jogger* for the information you need.

For now, fill in the date, your name, and circle the name of your *Reception* attribute. You will receive further instructions on how to fill out the rest of the form later.

When you have finished this, you may move on to *Page 101* (The white pages at the beginning of the Retention *attribute—How to use it* chapter).

LOGICAL MEMORY JOGGER

Date: _____

I am a Logical Learner   _____
                                                    name

RECEPTION   *(see page 43)*

I am (circle which you are) Auditory, Visual or Combination Language Processor.

REORGANIZATION   *(see page 57)*

Your Steps:

1. *Input Channel.* Use your best.

2. *Survey* the chapter asking yourself the two questions and write the major headings on separate pieces of paper.

3. *Read and organize.* Remember to use different colors for your main point, subpoints and your sub-subpoints.

4. *Scan* quickly over the chapter summary or study guide.

RETENTION   *(see page 101)*
Instructions will be given later for this section.

1. If I am a Musical Learner, I need to use music and rhythm when I am learning.
2. If I am a Body Kinesthetic Learner, I need to do something physical when I learn.
3. If I am talented in Knowing Self, I need to teach what I am learning to someone or something in order to experience what I am learning.
4. If I am talented in Knowing Others, I need to transform what I am learning into something concrete and real so that I can experience it.

MY PLAN:
1. During lecture I will:

2. When reading a textbook I will:

3. When studying for a test I will:

4. While taking a test I will:

Tear out along this perforated edge.

Spatial

Did you circle the compass? Then you are a *Spatial Learner*. You are a person who loves color and simplicity. You love knowing the bottom line. You will never understand a lecture until you know what the lecture is about. You learn best through pictures, maps, and drawings. You prefer *Figure 10* to *Figure 11*. Textbooks feel like *Figure 11*. Let me explain.

You may have noticed that when reading a textbook, you feel overwhelmed by all the words. Understanding is difficult even when you read the passage several times. You really wish they would just get to the point.

Linguistically talented people write textbooks and they love to use lots of words. Then they weave the information to make it more interesting for them, and this overwhelms the *Spatial Learner*. As a matter of fact, it can make one feel rather stupid.

You might find the following in a typical textbook. See if you can easily understand it.

> "Psychology may be defined as a scientific approach to the study of behavior. As a science, it brings carefully controlled methods of observation, such as the survey and the experiment, to bear on its subject matter whenever possible."

Did you understand it? Not really. A *Spatial* writer would have drawn a map, added color, and cut out most of the words. He would have found the flower like this:

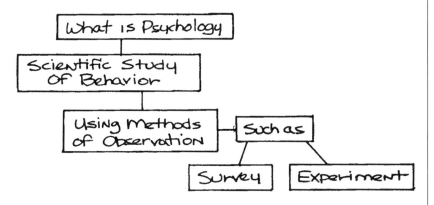

Isn't that better?

TO DO ★
Please get a piece of scratch paper and try your hand at *Mapping*. Find the essence of each sentence. I'll help.

Notice how each time you do this, you understand more of what was said.

Simplify

Figure 10

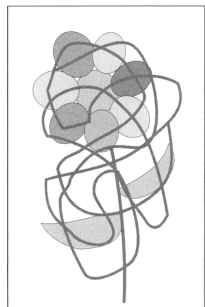
Figure 11

Here is a sentence you might find in a book:

- To be prejudiced in favor of our perceived interests entails that we become prejudiced against whomever or whatever appears to oppose or stand in the way of furthering them.

When you map it, it becomes:

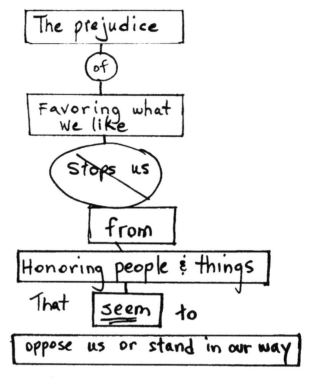

I remember things from eight weeks ago. This system really helps.

-So. California Nursing Student

Now, you try it.

Please map this on your sheet of paper:

- Listening is a difficult thing and it should be learned, honed, and nurtured if you want success.

Please map this on your sheet of paper:

- Most people believe that they listen quite well; they think they have a natural gift. They hear what is being said—the speaker's voice—but they fail to listen to the actual message.

Please map these on your sheet of paper:

- Some agreements are written in a vague manner, and if this is the case with your contract, you could accidentally give away some rights that you really intend to keep.

How did you do? Are the concepts easier to remember and understand? They should be. That's how you know if you are doing it correctly for you.

A SECOND THING THAT GETS IN YOUR WAY

Here is another thing, which I stated earlier, that gets in your way. *Linguistic* writers need to weave their writing.

Let me explain. In a textbook, you may encounter a major heading which reads, *The Goals of Psychology*. In your *Spatial Learner's* mind, you assume that the information under this heading will be exclusively about psychology's goals. In actuality, what you will find under this heading is a smorgasbord of ideas ranging from what psychologists do, studies they have performed, and of course, their goals. This absolutely confuses the *Spatial Learner's* mind.

Perhaps that is why you keep wasting your time rereading the chapter.

The *Spatial Reorganization* process you are about to learn will allow you to read your textbook one time, pull out what is important and put it into maps, and be done with your textbook.

USE DIFFERENT COLORED PENS

When making your maps, you will find it helpful to use *different* colored pens. These may be felt-tipped pens, colored pencils, or the four-colors-in-one pen. Experiment and see what you like best.

TO DO ★

Get some colored pens right now before you read on. Yellow might be a little light.

You will also find that using unlined larger than 81/2 x 11-inch paper will make your map-making more fun. Newsprint is good and less expensive. Give yourself space to express your creativity. Don't be afraid to let it all hang out.

There are four steps in the Spatial Reorganization process that you will follow when reading a textbook:

1. *Remember* to use your strongest *Reception* skill: *Auditory*, *Visual*, or *Combination*;

2. *Survey* the chapter;

3. *Map* the chapter;

4. *Scan* over the chapter summary and/or study guide.

I like using all the colors.

-So. California
Nursing Student

Graphic courtesy of Corel Corp.

I feel more confident since I have organized my notes better, and I feel the colors I use make a big difference. The colors make things stand out better.

-Pennsylvania
Nursing Student

When you feel overwhelmed by words, you can focus on a picture or a mandala like the one above, and it will bring you back to center.

FIRST STEP

Always *remember* to use your strongest *Reception* channel when you are reading. It will save you time and frustration. Use it!

SECOND STEP

Next, *Survey* the chapter. We talked earlier about how the *Linguistic* writer likes to weave their information.

As a *Spatial Learner*, the best way for you to cope with this is to *Survey* the major headings in each chapter so that you know what you are getting into.

This process, if done correctly, should take no more than five minutes per chapter. These five minutes will save you time in the long run. You *Survey* the chapter *quickly* by reading over the major headings and then asking yourself two quick questions, which you *will not* answer. The answers are not important. The beauty of this process is that it prepares your brain to receive information. It gets you interested in the subject matter. We only learn what we want to learn.

WHAT ARE THE MAJOR HEADINGS?

Major chapter headings are the *bold faced* headings that appear throughout a chapter. Most chapters have six or seven of these.

If you will look on the next page you will see the difference between major and minor headings. Usually the minor headings are in smaller print or in less bold print.

Once you have identified your major headings, read one heading at a time, asking yourself two quick questions about that heading, which you will not answer. Then write that heading at the top of a blank piece of paper. Look at our example on the opposite page.

The first major heading is: What Is Psychology? Read this heading and ask yourself a *Personal* and then a *Nonpersonal Question.*

THE QUESTIONS

A *personal question* is a question that relates to you personally. *My Personal Question*, for example, might be: "I wonder how this word came into existence?" Now you come up with your *Personal Question.*

Your second question has to be a *Nonpersonal Question*. A *Nonpersonal Question* is a question that is not personal to you.

WHAT IS PSYCHOLOGY? ←   — — — —

Psychology, like other sciences, seeks to describe,
explain,predict, and control the events it studies.

Major Headings

WHAT DO PSYCHOLOGISTS DO? ←

Psychologists share a keen interest in behavior, but in other
ways they may differ markedly.

Clinical Counseling Psychologists ←

Clincial psycholgists specialize in helpng people with
psychological problems adjust to the demands of life.

School and Educational Psychologists ←

School psychologists are empolyed by school systems to help
identify and assist students who encounter problems that
interfere with learning.

Minor Headings

Developmental Psycholgists ←

Developmental psycholgists study the changes—physical,
emotional, cognitve, and social—that occur throughout
the life span.

FAMOUS PSYCHOLOGISTS ←   — — — — —

Major Heading

Wilhelm Wundt ←

Wundt claimed that the mind was a natural event and could
be studied scienticially, just like sight, hearing, and the flow of
blood. He used the method of introspection, recommended by
Socrates, to try to discover the basic element of experience.

Minor Headings

William James ←

The brother of Henry James, William adopted a broader view
of psychhology that focused on the relation between conscious
experience and behavior. James was a major figure in the
development of psychology in the United States. He recieved
an MD degree from Harvard University but never practiced
medicine.

My Nonpersonal Question for that heading might be: "I wonder what kind of person becomes a psychologist?" Now it's your turn to make up your Nonpersonal Question.

Once you have asked your two questions, write the major heading at the top of a blank sheet of paper in one of the colors you were asked to get. Then put a box around the heading. (See next page.) The color you use will be your main point color. This is the beginning of your maps.

When you are finished with this step, you will have seven or eight sheets of paper with a single heading at the top of each page. The number of pages, of course, will be determined by the number of major headings in the chapter you are reading. I want to remind you that this step should take less than five minutes.

THE THIRD STEP

Now you are ready for the third step in the Reorganization process. The third step is to Map the chapter. We are going to take our examples from a psychology text.

As I said earlier, when you Survey the chapter, you have already begun this process by putting the major headings in boxes at the top of separate pieces of paper.

If you were to survey a chapter in a psychology textbook, you would have pages that look like this:

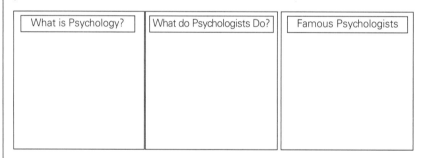

Mapping the chapter means distilling the important information down to its essence—finding the flower. The major headings that you put at the top of the pages during the Survey step will guide you as to what information is important. Once you have found these headings, your next step is to read the text and find the subpoints that tell you more about these major headings and then create maps with this information. Look at the following example on Page 90 to see how you do this.

What Is Psychology?   (write this in your main-point color)

SPATIAL REORGANIZATION EXAMPLE

Book Text	What to put on your paper	My Commentary

What is Psychology?

People love to watch people. Human beings are fascinated by human behavior. We surprise ourselves sometimes with just how interested we are. Psychologists are also intrigued by the mysteries of behavior and make an effort to answer questions such as *why* and *how*. But while most people try to satisfy their curiosity about behavior through casual observations, psychologists focus exclusively on studying human behavior.

Psychology is a scientific approach to the study of behavior. As a science, it brings carefully controlled methods of observation, such as the survey and the experiment, to bear on its subject whenever possible. Human behavior is the biggest interest of most psychologists; however, many of them focus much or all of their research on the behavior of animals, ranging from rats and pigeons to flatworms and gorillas.

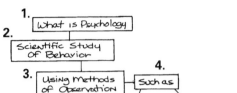

1. Your heading has been determined for you during the survey step.

2. This is your first sub-point. It tells you more about *What is Psychology.*

3. Next you further define *What is Psychology* with this phrase.

4. Finally, you tell more about the observations. (Please notice that the ideas were distilled down considerably without losing the original meaning.)

As you read on, you will find other important ideas which you will want to extract. For example: "Human behavior is the biggest interest of most psychologists..." Where do you put this? You put this under the heading, *What Do Psychologists Do?* not under *What is Psychology?*

Please look at the next four pages. These are examples of maps that were done by my students. They were originally made using many colors—so use your imagination. These examples are presented to encourage you to be as creative as you wish with your own *Mapping.* Let it all hang out—you will have more fun. When finished, go to *Page 101* and read the last step.

examples: eating 8
noting, involuntary
bodily functions

mental processes must
be based on self-
report of the person
experiencing them

strong emotions
are accompanied by
increases in heart
rate and breathing

The Goals Of
Psychotherapy

seeks to describe, explain
predict and control event
it studies

describe and explain
behavior by learing,
motivation, emotion, intelligence, personality and attitudes

direct terms and
concepts are interwoven
into theories

related set of statements
about events

allow us to
desire explanations
and predictions

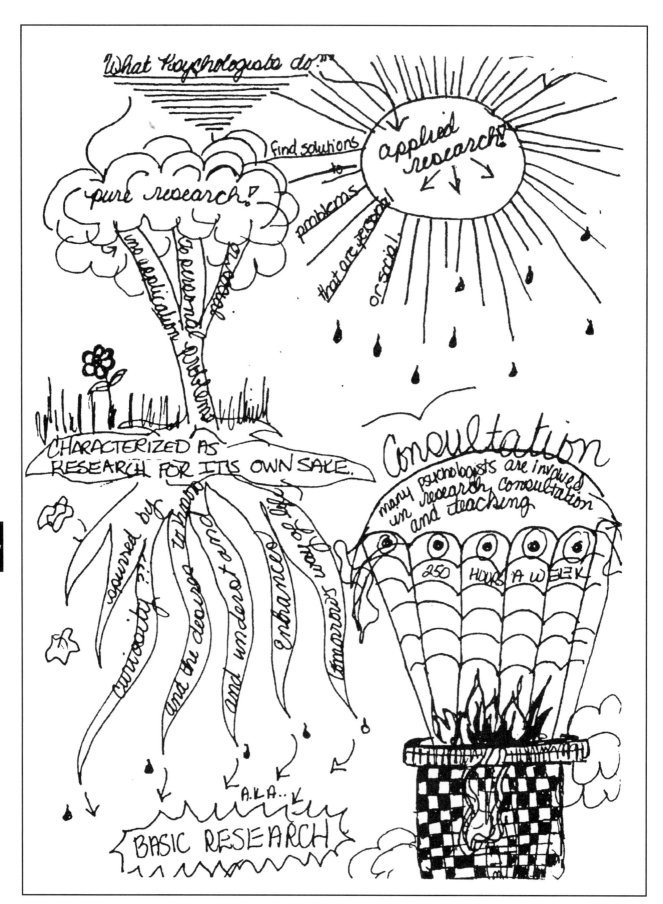

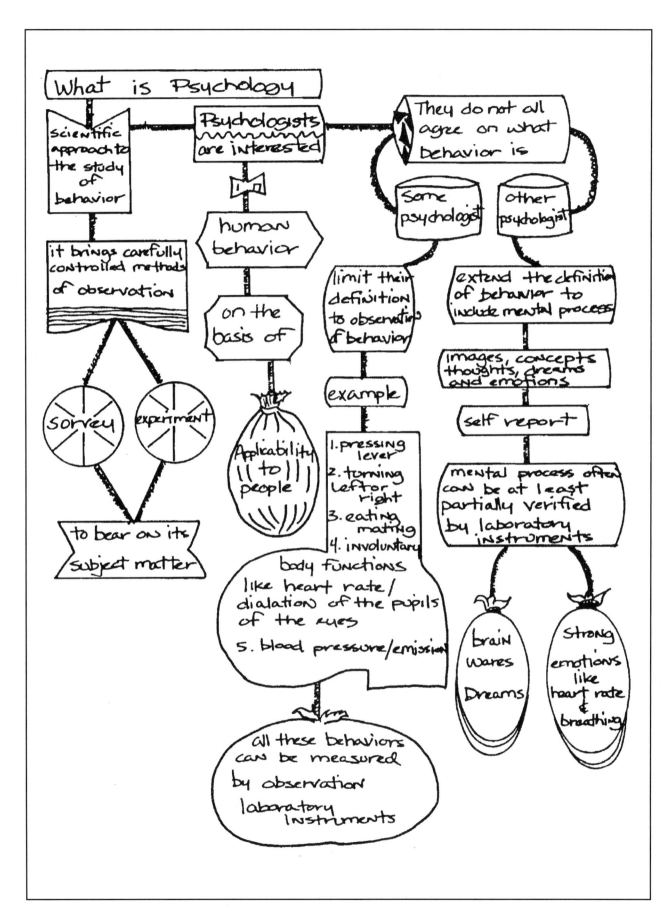

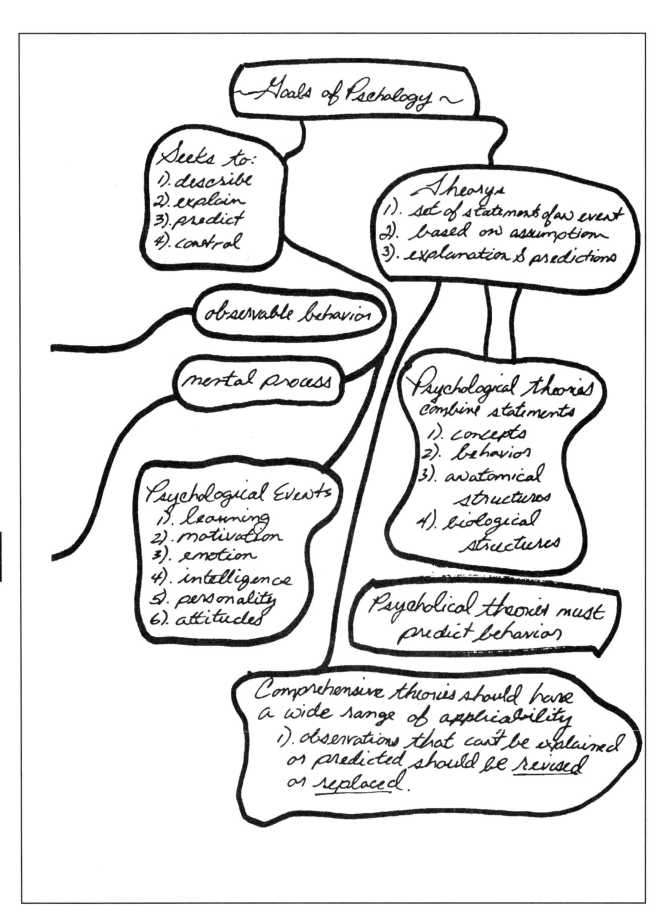

THE LAST STEP

The final step in the *Reorganization Process* is to *Scan* the chapter summary and study guide. This step involves the fast reading of the study guide or chapter summary.

Many of my students tell me that they study the wrong things for tests. The *Survey* and *Mapping* steps should help you with this.

However, it is also helpful to *quickly* read over the chapter summary or study guide to make sure that you included all important information.

If something is in the chapter summary or study guide, it will probably be on the test. Chapter summaries are usually found at the end of the chapters, but sometimes they are at the beginning. Study guides usually come with most textbooks, but not all instructors order them. They can usually be purchased at the school's bookstore. If you find information that doesn't look familiar, immediately go to the source in the chapter, and include this information in your maps.

This concludes the overview of the four steps of the *Spatial Reorganization* process.

The following is an expanded example of how you should *Spatially Reorganize* your chapter. In real life you should use many colors. For this demonstration only black, white, and gray will be used. The excerpts are taken from *Men Are From Mars and Women Are From Venus*, by John Gray, Ph.D.

Review this material carefully so that you will be able to imitate the process while you are reading a textbook.

*Just before reading the **YASTYT** book, I had failed the last two out of three exams. After reading this book and applying the ideas, I passed my next two exams and my final exam with flying colors. I ended up with a B for the class!*

-Southern CA
Nursing Student

SPATIAL REORGANIZATION EXAMPLE

Book Text

LIFE ON MARS

Martians value power, competency, efficiency, and achievement. They are always doing things to prove them-selves and develop their power and skills. Their sense of self is defined through their ability to achieve results. They experience fulfillment primarily through success and accomplishment. Everything on Mars is a reflection of these values. Even their dress is designed to reflect their skills and competence. Police officers, soldiers, businessmen, scientists, cab drivers, technicians, and chefs all wear uniforms or at least hats to reflect their competence and power.

They don't read magazines like Psychology Today, Self, or People. They are more concerned with outdoor activities like hunting, fishing, and racing cars. They are interested in the news, weather, and sports and couldn't care less about romance novels and self-help books.

They are more interested in objects and things rather than people and feelings. Even today on earth, while women fantasize about romance, men fantasize about powerful cars, faster computers, gadgets, gizmos, and new, more powerful technology. Men are preoccupied with the things that can help them express power by creating results and achieving their goals.

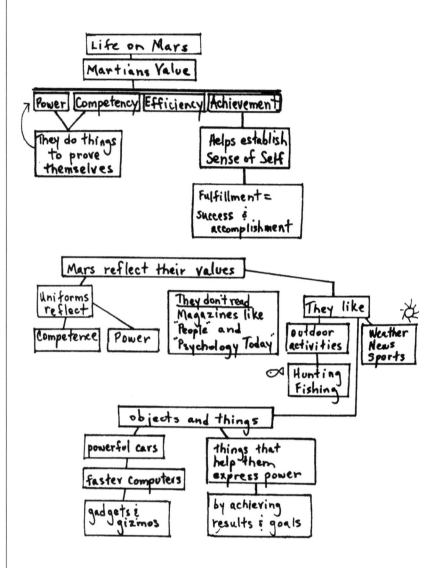

Men Are From Mars and Women Are From Venus
Copyright © 1992 by John Gray
Reprinted by permission of HarperCollinsPublishers, Inc.

SPATIAL REORGANIZATION EXAMPLE

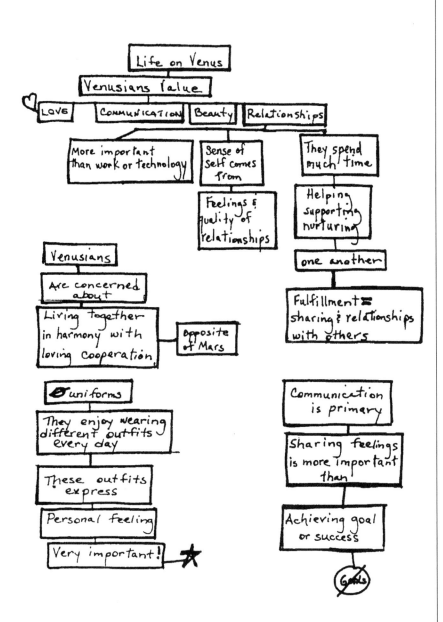

Men Are From Mars and Women Are From Venus
Copyright © 1992 by John Gray
Reprinted by permission of HarperCollinsPublishers, Inc.

Book Text

LIFE ON VENUS

Venusians have different values. They value love, communication, beauty, and relationships. They spend a lot of time supporting, helping, and nurturing one another. Their sense of self is defined through their feelings and the quality of their relationships. They experience fulfillment through sharing and relating.

Everything on Venus reflects these values. Rather than building highways and tall buildings, the Venusians are more concerned with living together in harmony, community, and loving cooperation. Relationships are more important than work and technology. In most ways their world is the opposite of Mars.

They do not wear uniforms like the Martians (to reveal their competence). On the contrary, they enjoy wearing a different outfit every day, according to how they are feeling. Personal expression, especially of their feelings is very important. They may even change outfits several times a day as their mood changes.

Communication is of primary importance. To share their personal feelings is much more important than achieving goals and success. Talking and relating to one another is a source of tremendous fulfillment.

THE SPATIAL MEMORY JOGGER

You are now ready for the *Retention step*.

Before you turn to these pages please turn to the next page. There you will find your *Memory Jogger*. This sheet is designed to jog your memory. If you forget a step while you are studying, you can refer to this sheet.

This system is simple and it is easy to drop a step. The *Memory Jogger* is a tool you can use constantly to keep yourself on track. If you need help on a particular step, go to the page numbers listed on your *Memory Jogger* for the information you need. Tear it out and use it!

For now, fill in the date, your name, and circle the name of your *Reception* attribute. You will receive further instructions on how to fill out the rest of the form later.

When you have finished this, you may move on to *Page 101* (the *white pages* at the beginning of the *Retention—How to use it* chapter).

SPATIAL MEMORY JOGGER

Date: _____

I am a Spatial Learner   _____
                                            name

RECEPTION   (*see page 43*)

I am (circle which you are) Auditory, Visual or Combination Language Processor.

REORGANIZATION   (*see page 57*)

> Your Steps:
>
> > **1.** *Remember* to use your best *Reception* channel.
> >
> > **2.** *Survey*. (Don't forget the questions.)
> >
> > **3.** *Map the chapter*.
> >
> > **4.** *Scan* the chapter summary or study guide.

RETENTION   (*see page 101*)

Instructions will be given later for this section.

1. If I am a Musical Learner, I need to use music and rhythm when I am learning.
2. If I am a Body Kinesthetic Learner, I need to do something physical when I learn.
3. If I am talented in Knowing Self, I need to teach what I am learning to someone or something in order to experience what I am learning.
4. If I am talented in Knowing Others, I need to transform what I am learning into something concrete and real so that I can experience it.

MY PLAN:
1. During lecture I will:

2. When reading a textbook I will:

3. When studying for a test I will:

4. While taking a test I will:

Retention attribute
How to use it

He only is exempt from failures who makes no efforts.
—Dennis Whately

1. *In this chapter you will learn how to retain information instead of just memorizing it.*

2. *This will save you lots of time.*

3. *You may find some of the ideas a little scary because they fly in the face of everything you have ever been taught.*

4. *The exercises are designed to alleviate some of this fear.*

5. *Your honesty will make a difference.*

A few years ago, I was riding on an airplane and I began talking with a lady sitting next to me. She asked me what I did for a living and I told her. She then proceeded to tell me about her six-year-old grandson. She was pleased to say that he could count to 100. However, he was unable to answer questions like, "Is five before or after four?" All he could do was sequentially repeat the numbers from 1-100.

This is an excellent example of one kind of short-term learning. It is commonly referred to as *memorizing*. It is static memory. You can't manipulate it in any way. Some of you know this kind of memory intimately. It has gotten you through years of true or false and multiple choice exams.

The problem with memorizing is that Retention is short term—usually held long enough to pass the test. It is nonflexible. All you can do is repeat in a rote manner what you have memorized. Any changes will throw you. In addition, it also takes about one-third more time to memorize something than to learn it in long-term memory, using the **YASTYT** system.

This chapter is about *Retention*, not memorization. When you truly retain the numbers from 1-100, they come alive. They are no longer a rote, unconnected string. You can manipulate them. You can add and subtract them. You can use them.

TO DO ★
Right now, without looking back, try to recall as much of the information that was *Reorganized* for you from the *Men Are From Mars and Women Are From Venus* selection.

What are the characteristics of people from Mars? Just for the fun of it, see how many you can name.

Illustration F

What are the characteristics of people from Venus? Again, see how many you can come up with.

Now go back and check to see how many you got correct.

You remembered quite a number, didn't you? Surprised? The reason this occurred is that you have been using your brain the way it was designed to be used. Much of this information which you just remembered is now in your long-term memory. How often has this happened after one reading of a textbook? Not very often, I'll bet. How many times do you usually reread a chapter? The following *Retention* step is meant to get the rest of the information into long-term memory without memorization.

Retention occurs when information hops onto one or two of your best neurological pathways and is then carried directly into long-term memory. Remember, I talked about this in *Chapter 1*. I also referred to it when I told you the story of the farmer and the sheep. When he took his sheep to the barn, the farmer took the most direct route (*See Illustration F*). This is also what you want to do with the information you want to learn.

Please look at your *Personal Learning Summary*. You will see a list of attributes under the section labeled *Retention*. You will also see that you have circled two or three of the icons next to your strongest attributes. These circled attributes are your vehicles for retaining information expediently.

FAITH IS BELIEVING IN SOMETHING YOU CANNOT SEE

Throughout this book, you have been reading comments from students like yourself. They have been placed along the way to help you with your faith. Why? Do I really believe your faith to be that poor? No. It has to do with something I have discovered about many people. Many of us have learned erroneously from early school experiences that good students learn by reading silently, highlighting or taking notes, and then reviewing the material again and again until the material is memorized. Anything other than this is just not a good study habit. To do something different seems scary just because it is new and goes against an established belief.

Doing things differently confronts our very sense of security. As you go through this section, if you can be honest with yourself about how you are feeling, the feelings will dissipate. In support of this, periodically you will be asked to express how you are feeling at that moment. This is your opportunity to say anything you want. Use it. It will help you to get through this section and apply this program to your own learning process.

The things you will now be asked to do fly in the face of

My study time has been reduced by three-quarters. I feel like my stress level is drastically decreased, also because I know I will do well.

-Pennsylvania
Nursing Student

everything you have ever been told about good study habits. Don't let your fears invalidate their value to you. These techniques are not unorthodox to your brain. We have been kidding ourselves into believing that we all learn the same way. But we now know that our brains are more different than our fingerprints.

The student comments that you have been reading throughout this book are real comments from real students like yourself. Trust them and then trust yourself.

I had a student majoring in nursing a few years ago who became an A student and passed her boards the first time she took them. She danced while she studied. Not very conventional? No, but it didn't stop her. She continued to dance and continued to reap the benefits. The benefits occurred because the dancing and music stimulated her strong pathways —*Music* and *Body Kinesthetic*; and the information was thus moved directly to her long-term memory. You will get to experience the power of this in a minute.

TO DO ★

What are your feelings at this moment? Do you feel a little uneasy? Would you feel funny if you had to dance and study at the same time? Write something on a scrap of paper— anything such as: "I feel scared. I don't know what I feel. I feel overwhelmed. I feel angry that I have to read this book. This stuff seems strange. I resent being in this situation." Write something.

You will notice that the nursing student, mentioned above, blended two activities and made them into one. Dancing is a *Musical* activity and it is also a *Body Kinesthetic* activity. You will be doing a similar thing with two of your strong attributes. It may not be dancing and singing but something that feels more akin to you.

PLEASE REMEMBER THIS

I want to add that it is important during this *Retention* process that you use your best *Reception* skill. Remember our farmer? He couldn't get in to the pen without first opening the gate. Your brain's gate needs to be open if you want to retain anything. That means if you are an *Auditory Language Processor* you must use your tape player and listen. If you are a *Visual Language Processor* you must read silently and if you are a *Combination Language Processor* you must read aloud. Please factor these elements into the suggestions made.

You are now ready to learn how to utilize your *Retention* attributes. Earlier you should have circled two icons on your *Personal Learning Summary*, *Page 17*, under the *Retention*

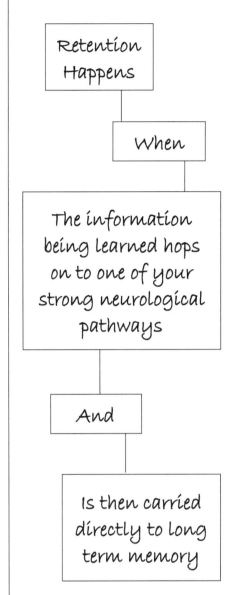

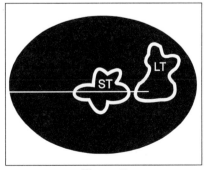

Figure 5

category. Please look at your *Personal Learning Summary* now, and note which two icons you circled. Then turn to the icon-coded pages that correspond to the icons you circled. Remember, all you are doing is stimulating your strong neurological pathways so that the information can get on these pathways and go directly to long-term memory. It is not anything more or less than this.

Musical

If you circled the treble clef icon, you are a *Musical Learner.* You love rhythm. In order to use your musical neurological pathway you must stimulate it with rhythm. How? Try this. Right now start singing the song, *Mary Had A Little Lamb*, to yourself. Do it. Next, hum it. Now, get rid of the words. Keep humming.

In the front of this book (*Page iv*), about three-quarters of the way down, you will find the *ISBN Number*. Now sing this number to the music you have been humming. Sing it a couple of times. Good. Stop singing. We will come back to this in a minute.

As I said, you learn best when rhythm is present. Rhythm can be used while studying in several different ways. At the end of this chapter I will tell you how students of mine have used the following ideas successfully. For now, here are some possibilities you may wish to consider:

1. If you play a musical instrument by ear, you can play this instrument while you review the material you want to learn. Make sure that playing the instrument is not your primary focus.

2. You can beat out rhythms with your hand or a stick as you say what you want to learn to that rhythm. Rap the information.

3. You can play classical instrumental background music as you study. You may use other instrumental music— all except rock. Rock will hinder your learning. It is not good for brain cells. I like to change the music depending on the mood I am in and the subject or activity I am doing.

4. Just as we did above, you can remove the words to a song that you know well, and put what you want to learn into their place. Just as we did above.

Now, get the song, *Mary Had A Little Lamb*, going in your head again. Sing the numbers you just learned and write them on a piece of paper. Go back and check to see if you got the number correct. Isn't that exciting? This happened simply because you stimulated one of your strong neurological pathways and it went right to long-term memory. When you wake up tomorrow morning get *Mary Had A Little Lamb* going in your head again and notice how quickly you retrieve the number.

Soft music in the background has really helped me retain what I have to learn.

-Ohio
Nursing Student

One student of mine played the guitar very well. He could play without thinking. When he studied, he would play the guitar and sing what he had to learn. He was a straight A science major.

TO DO ★

From now on, I want you to utilize this pathway while you read the rest of this book. Find a classical music station or put on some instrumental music. Music with words will compete with what you are reading, so don't use it. Experiment with the volume. As the music is playing, notice how it calms and focuses you. If you circled this icon, use music. It will be your ticket to success.

Does this technique seem strange? What are you feeling? How are you feeling right now? See if you can write about what you are feeling on a piece of scrap paper. Please try to do this. It will help you. Write: Right now I feel . . .

Please turn to your next *Reception* attribute and read about it. If you are finished, turn to *Page 121* to find out how to blend these attributes.

Body Kinesthetic

If you circled the gymnast icon, you are a *Body Kinesthetic Learner*. You love to move. You love to use your body. You feel better when you have used your body. In order to trigger your *Body Kinesthetic* neurological pathway, you must move while you learn. How? Some of you may recall a time when you were studying and got up from where you were sitting to get a drink of water and suddenly what you were studying was remembered or understood.

You are also a person who doesn't do well sitting still for long periods. In class, I recommend that you bounce your leg or tap your finger quietly on the desk. Any movement will keep you alert and help you comprehend more effectively. Please be mindful of the speaker and other students. Large movements and noise can be very distracting.

If you want to increase your reading comprehension, you can move your fingers under the words you, or you can grab both sides of the book or paper you are reading.

Most people find that when studying, large muscle movements works better than small movements such as typing or writing. However for some people, writing and typing works well. You will have to discover what is true for you. Here are some possibilities you may wish to consider:

1. Do anything physical while you review what you want to learn. This can be just walking around the room, washing the dishes, riding a stationary bike, or exercising. Don't make the motor activity the primary focus of your attention.

2. If you happen to be *Musical*, you could dance or move to the rhythm.

TO DO ★

As you read the rest of this book, I want you to use this idea. If you can sit so that you can swing your leg while you read, do so. If you have a rocking chair, that will also work. If not, read for a short time and then get up and walk around. Notice how these actions calm you and help you to focus. If you circled this icon, movement is your ticket to success. Use it

What are you feeling now? Does this technique seem strange? Can you see yourself doing this movement during study time? Please write what you are feeling on a piece of scrap paper now.

Please turn to your next *Retention* attribute and read about it. If you are complete, turn to *Page 121* to find out how to blend these attributes.

One of my students was a jazzercise instructor. She was studying nursing and was a single mom. She did not have a great deal of spare time. She was *Body Kinesthetically* talented so she jazzercised while she studied. She made it through nursing with time to spare.

Graphics this page courtesy of Corel Corp.

Knowing Self

If you circled the heart with an arrow pointing inward icon, you are an introspective person. You view the world in terms of yourself. You know what you want, what you like, and what is important to you. You are an *Experiential Knowing Self Learner*. Your strong neurological pathway gets stimulated when you experience information, rather than just reading about it.

WHAT DO I MEAN BY EXPERIENCING INFORMATION?

Let's say you needed to learn how to change the spark plugs in a car. If you went out and played around with the spark plugs and eventually figured out how to change them, you would have experienced the information. If you had only read about how to do it in a manual, you would not have experienced it. Do you see the difference?

Because you are talented in *Knowing Self*, information becomes Experiential for you when you teach it to someone or something else. It can be the wall, the dog, the air, anything. The simple act of teaching a concept gives you an experience of it. Whenever you experience information, it will hop onto your strong neurological pathway and go directly to long-term memory.

You can use this to your advantage. You would make a wonderful study group leader. Just through the simple act of teaching all your friends, you will learn almost instantly.

TO DO ★

Right now, I want you to get into a teaching mode as you read the rest of this book. Notice how this simple change in attitude makes understanding so much easier. So teach. It is your ticket to success.

What are you feeling now? Risk? How does this word make you feel? Do you like to risk with your grades? Tell me how you are feeling. I want to know. Please write what you can on a scrap of paper.

Now, turn to your next *Retention* attribute and read about it. When you are finished, turn to Page 121 to find out how to blend these attributes.

When one of my students discovered she was talented in *Knowing Self* and an *Experiential Learner*, she formed a study group. She was the leader and she taught all of her friends anatomy and physiology. When the class was over, everyone involved had passed with A's.

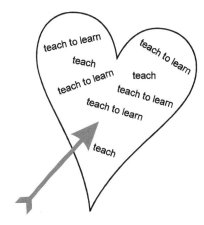

Knowing Others

If you circled the heart with an arrow pointing outward icon, you are a person very in tune with others. You understand by perceiving outside yourself. You read people and situations easily. You are what we call an *Experiential Knowing Others Learner*. Your strong neurological pathway gets stimulated when you experience a piece of information rather than just reading about it.

You might read the following definition for the word *displacement*:

"Displacement is the difference between a later position of a thing and its original position."

You may think you understand this definition, but you will not remember nor fully understand it because it is too abstract. You can make it more concrete by simply doing a demonstration of displacement.

A demonstration would involve getting a glass of water filled halfway full, then sticking a spoon into the glass and watching the water rise. When you see the water rise and experience the way the spoon displaces the water, you will have experienced displacement. (*See Figure 12*.) You will understand its meaning at a deep level. This experience of displacement will go immediately to long-term memory and you will be able to answer any question about it.

Most information moves along a continuum from abstract to concrete. (*See Figure 13*.)

Any information can be made more concrete. As an *Experiential Knowing Others Learner*, you will want to transform abstract information into something more concrete, so that you can experience it and learn it easily.

Here is another example of how you can do this. Let's say that you had to learn the information in the following paragraph:

Abuse in the family is most frequently inflicted by the father. It usually begins with a child when he is about age four, and continues until age 12. The abuse from the father is his way of claiming control and power. The mother usually denies that the abuse is happening, and this makes the child very angry.

There are a number of pieces of information in this paragraph, and just to remember them will never work for the *Experiential Learner*. What will work, though, is a picture story that can be acted out, drawn out, or visualized, giving you an experience of the information.

Figure 12

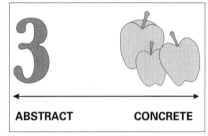

ABSTRACT   **CONCRETE**

Figure 13

The **YASTYT** book helped me more than the Student Success class.

-Wisconsin
Nursing Student

Figure 14

I am studying less and getting better grades. Since this is a difficult class, I feel good that I am making it.

-Southern CA
Nursing Student

This is how I would visualize it: the abuse is carried out by the father, who uses it for control and power. So, I see a father with large muscles, holding onto a rope tied around a child's neck. The child is on his hands and knees, on the floor. The large muscles and the rope around the child's neck are labeled with the words *power* and *control.* On the front of the child I see the numbers 4-12, which are the ages when abuse usually takes place. Then, I see the mother standing on the other side of the child with her hands over her eyes. She is peeking through her fingers at the situation. This signifies that she knows, but doesn't want to know. The child looks back at the mother with an angry face. He does this because her denial really makes him mad. (*See Figure 14.*)

If you were able to see this scene as you read it, you had an experience. If you were to look away, you could repeat back any of the information in the paragraph just by recalling the picture. You could do it now, and you could do it ten days from now. You could write a paragraph just from the information in this picture. You have experienced it, so it is in long-term memory. This is so much faster than trying to review and review and review the information. One or two times thinking about this picture and this information is yours.

I recommend that when you begin this *Experiential* process, you work with a partner. Two heads are better than one when you begin. You will be able to come up with ideas a lot faster, and both of you will benefit.

The two of you can brainstorm ideas and scenarios that will give you experiences for the different pieces of information you must learn. Once you come up with the experience, you will learn the information almost instantly, and it will be in your long-term memory.

Experiential Learners can't be passive. You must be involved in what you are learning. You must discover a compelling reason for learning what you are learning.

Here are some ideas you may wish to incorporate:
1. In chemistry, biology, physics, or physiology—any of the sciences—do an experiment or imagine one in your head. (Examples: Imagine what happens when you combine sulfur with ammonia. See the elements combine. If you are learning the parts of the body, see the body in front of you, or draw it and feel the parts in your own body. Let yourself experience what you are learning. If your school has a learning lab, use it.

A student that I met last year told me that she had created an *Experiential* periodical chart.)

2. In foreign language classes, act out the words you are trying to learn. Label items or draw pictures of items and put the foreign name on them. Set up a situation and have a conversation with a friend, using the vocabulary you want to learn.

3. In history, you may imagine that you are one of the Generals on a battlefield and you view the whole war from this one man's perspective or experience. Make it real for yourself. Make the people you are learning about real. Make a time line for dates. Make the places that you must learn about very personal to you. You can do the same thing in literature classes.

4. In political science or psychology class, relate what you must learn to your own life. Pretend that you are a politician and learn things from a very personal perspective. In psychology, make the information personal to you. Relate the information to something you already know and care about in your family. Relate what you are learning to your own experiences at home or at work.

5. In math, you must understand the theory behind the problems. Most mathematicians will understand the theory by doing the problem. It comes to them through the act of doing the problem. It helps you greatly to know the theory up front. For example, you should understand why you are learning algebra. You can figure out algebraic questions without using algebra, but algebra makes it easier and faster. Once you have understood this, learning algebra will be a whole lot simpler.

   Doing lots of problems will help you understand the theory also. Most instructors do not give you enough homework to accomplish this. You will have to do more on your own. Make understanding the theory your goal. Look for ways to turn everything that is abstract into something concrete.

6. To help you with any of the above you can create *Memory Cue Cards*. These cards are designed to give you an experience of what you are learning. They can help move an abstract piece of information, such as a math formula, to something more concrete. If you come up with a meaningful idea, you will learn the information very quickly. Create these cards with

your friends. Creating will go much faster and you will have more fun. Please turn to the next page for some examples. The easiest way to make these cards is to use colored pens and index cards. I prefer the large-sized cards. It is helpful if you keep the number of items on each card at a minimum. You can do a variety of things that I will show on the following pages. Drawing pictures is one way you can move something from abstract to concrete.

Memory Cue Cards

On these *six* pages, you will find some examples of *Memory Cue Cards* made by my students. Look them over to help yourself better understand this idea. When you are finished looking at these *Memory Cue Cards*, please turn to *Page 121* for your next step in *Blending* these *Reception* attributes.

ABBREVIATIONS MADE EASY

Let's say that you want to learn a series of abbreviations for use in note taking. These little abstract symbols, when combined with a concrete concept, can be learned very quickly. B/T is the abbreviation for between. If you place it *between* something as we have done in our example, you will be able to remember it much faster than if you just listed it and tried to memorize it.

Use RED for the abbreviations

Use other colors for drawings

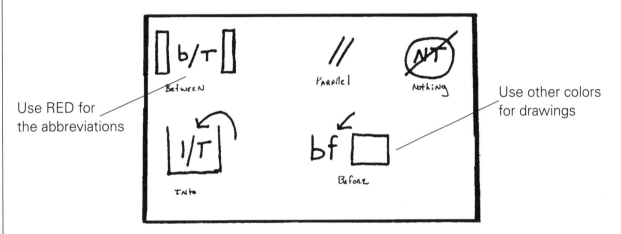

On the following cards, we are relating something we know to something we are wanting to learn. This card happens to be relating dish washing to the way a computer processes information.

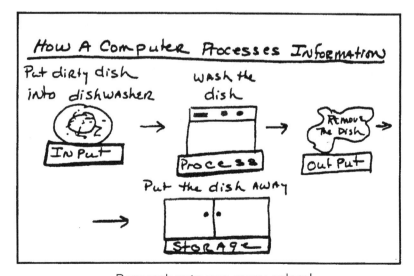

Remember to use many colors!

Imagine using many bright colors!

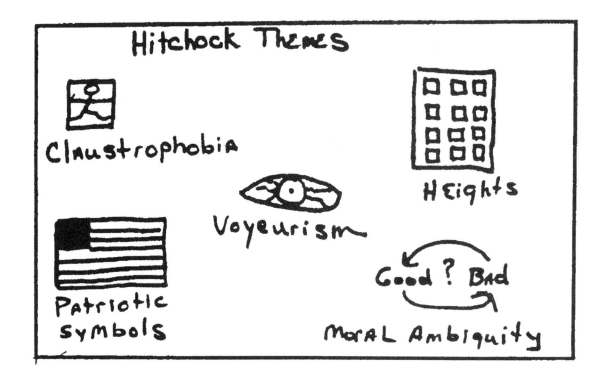

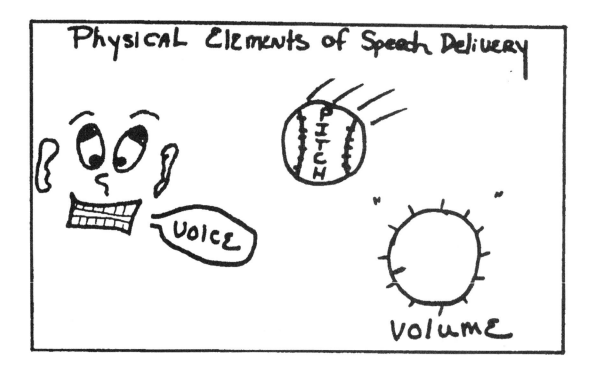

Pictures always work well. So does using many different colors!

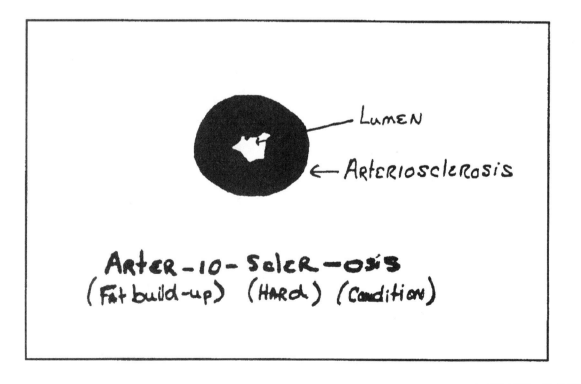

Don't forget to visualize and use color!

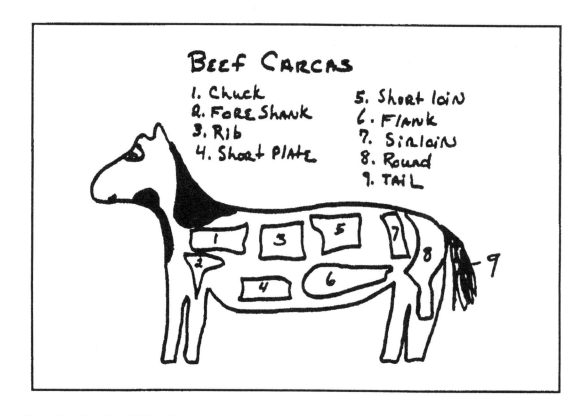

You can even make abstract math concepts more concrete
by drawing pictures. Using color is also very helpful.

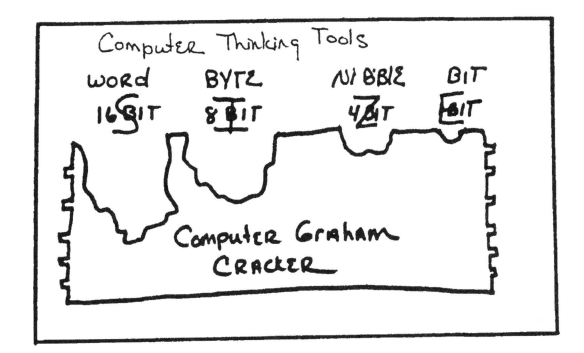

Mnemonic devices also work well. For the first few days, learn a story constructed from first letters of the words you want to learn.

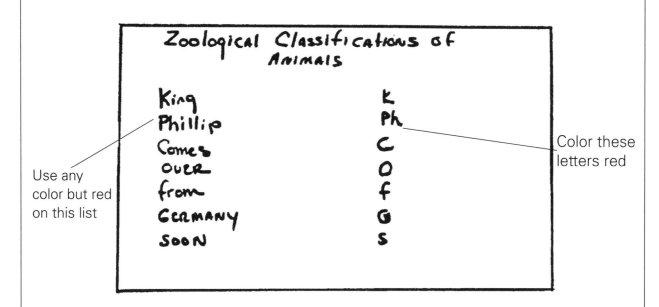

Use any color but red on this list

Color these letters red

When you have learned the story, put in the words you want to learn. You will be surprised how fast you learn this material.

BLENDING

Before I show you how to blend your *Retention* attributes, I want to digress for a moment and give you an opportunity, again, to express some of your feelings. I know you have been doing this periodically. Now, I want you to really express your most honest feelings. The emphasis here is on being negative. I want to hear about how you *really* feel. I want you to be as critical as you have ever been. I want you to air your complaints. I want you to go for the throat. I want this to be a feeding frenzy. This is not about being nice. I want to hear your complaints, your criticisms, your concerns, your reasons for inaction, everything.

Next, write down the words that complete these phrases:

I was happy to learn some new techniques. I loaned my book to several friends who also enjoyed it. In fact, I need to get it back to reread some areas.

-Pennsylvania
Nursing Student

TO DO ★

Example: 1. One of the things I hate about this system is <u>everything</u>.

2. A second thing I hate about this system is_____

_____.

3. One thing I don't like about doing things differently is _____

_____.

4. A second thing I don't like about doing things differently is_____.

5. These techniques (be really negative) _____

_____.

6. These techniques (be even more negative) _____

_____.

7. These techniques (let it all hang out—no one is going to read this)_____

_____.

8. Risking is _____.

9. Risking is _____.

10. Risking is _____.

11. My instructors are _____.

12. My instructors are _____.

13. I am angry because _____.

14. This learning system makes me angry because _____

_____.

15. This activity _____.

16. I hate _____.

17. I hate even more _____.

18. One thing that makes me mad is _____.

19. Another thing that makes me mad is _____.

20. I wish _____.

21. Do you really think this system will save you time? _____.

22. Why won't it save you time? _____

Good. Thank you for your honesty. I hope this made you feel better.

Now, I would like you to be very positive. I want you to write about what good things you see in this learning system. What do you feel excited about trying? How do you envision that it will help you? What good do you see about this program?

_____

_____

_____

Now you are ready to continue.

HOW TO BLEND

You have just learned how to get information into long-term memory by stimulating your strong neurological pathways. In order to maximize this *Retention* process, you will want to blend two of your abilities whenever possible. This means if you are *Musical* and *Body Kinesthetic*, you will want to move to a rhythm, and maybe even sing what you are trying to learn. Here are more stories to help you come up with your way to retain.

Story One

My very first student was talented *Musically*, and she was *Body Kinesthetic* and *Auditory*. She had a very big anatomy test coming up. I suggested that she put the information she had to learn on tape (*Auditory*). She played the piano by ear, so I asked her to listen to the tape while she played the piano (*Musical* and *Body Kinesthetic*). She listened to the tape one time through, and then she had her parents test her on the material. Much to her surprise, she had learned the material completely. Most people will have to review their material two or three times, which is much less than what most of you have been doing in the past.

Story Two

A young man who had flunked out of high school several times came to me. We found out that he was *Body Kinesthetic*, *Knowing Others*, and a *Combination Learner*. He made *Memory Cue Cards* for the information he had to learn (*Knowing Others*) He went outside and read the cards aloud (*Combination*) as he kicked his soccer ball against the garage (*Body Kinesthetic*). He was a real soccer fan. In less than a month, he had pulled his grades up from D's and F's to A's and B's.

I definitely feel better about my study skills, and I feel very confident about going into Nursing 100 in the fall. I am actually looking forward to learning my new material in a different way.

-Pennsylania
Nursing Student

Story Three

I had a college student who was a *Musical, Knowing Others*, and *Visual Language Processor*. She was learning the history of the Civil War. She loved movies and pretended that she was one of the field marshals during the Civil War (*Knowing Others*). She read over what she wanted to learn and imagined herself on the battlefield (*Visual* and *Knowing Others*). As she did this, she tapped out the rhythm to the *Battle Hymn of the Republic* (*Musical*). She never got anything less than the highest A.

Story Four

Another one of my nursing students was a *Musical, Knowing Self*, and *Combination Learner*. She led a study group (*Knowing Self*). She had a very large chalkboard that she used to teach her fellow students (*Combination*). She had background music playing and, occasionally, would use rhythm to help teach a difficult concept (*Musical*). She got very high A's, and her students did well too.

Story Five

My last example is a student who was also the leader of her study group. She was *Body Kinesthetic, Knowing Self*, and *Auditorily* talented. She led a unique study group (*Knowing Self*). She led it while she used her exercise bike (*Body Kinesthetic*). She taught everything from that bike. She had a *Combination Learner* friend write things on a board; however, she focused just on being aural. She did everything aloud (*Auditory*). Again, everyone did very well.

THIS IS IMPORTANT

I want to make an important point here. Internalizing is not memorizing. You do not have to go over and over a piece of information to remember it if you are doing it correctly. One or two times and you should have it. I recommend that you review a section of material you want to learn, using the internalization techniques, and then test yourself to see how much you have actually learned. Don't kid yourself. You know when you know something. As you get more confident with this system, this process will happen even faster.

Dear Renée,

Thirty-seven years ago I was 21 and dropped out of college because I was a lousy student.

I enrolled in school last summer for the first time since then. I am taking 60 units of undergraduate science required before I can go on to obtain my Masters of Chinese Medicine degree. I never took the pre-med science classes before because I did so poorly in science when I was in high school.

A friend steered me to your book, You are Smarter than You Think! I read it, took the self-test to discover my own best methods of acquiring information, applied them in my studies, and got a 4.0 in the Psychology class I took l ast summer.

I'm currently a full-time student, carrying 11 units in addition to working full-time. My class load this semester includes Biology, Nutrition, English, and Library Science.

I'm maintaining three A's and one B. It would be impossible for me without the study methods acquired from you. Thank you.

These last two words, thank you, are inadequate to express the breadth and depth of my appreciation. They'll have to do until I can come up with something better.

Sincerely,

James Speck

MEMORY JOGGER

Please refer to your *Memory Jogger*. If you are *Linguistically* talented, and you your forgot to tear out that page, do so now. You'll find it on *Page 69*. If you are *Logically* talented, turn to *Page 82*, and if you are *Spatially* talented, turn to Page 99.

It is time for you to come up with your own plan.

If you still feel unsure about what to do, go to the *Application Chart* in *Appendix C*. Look up your attributes and look across. It will instruct you generally as to what you can do in all basic learning situations. As you get more comfortable with this system, I suggest you personalize what you do. It will make it more fun.

Now look at your *Memory Jogger*.

On the bottom of the sheet, you will see the *Retention* section. On your *Personal Learning Summary* sheet, if you circled the treble clef icon, you are a *Musical Learner*; the gymnastic icon, you are a *Body Kinesthetic Learner*; the heart with the arrow pointing into the icon, you are an *Experiential Knowing Self Learner*; the heart with the arrow pointing out, you are an *Experiential Knowing Others Learner*.

On your *Memory Jogger*, please circle your best attributes under the *Retention* section. Most of you will have two attributes circled, and some of you may have three.

At the bottom of the *Memory Jogger*, under *My Plan*, please write down your plan for how you will transform learning during *Lecture*, *Textbook Reading*, *Test Studying*, and *Test Taking*. You will write something like this for Test Studying:

"I will create Memory Cue Cards and then review the material aloud while I walk around." (This person is a *Combination*, *Body Kinesthetic*, and *Experiential Learner*.)

The only people who never fail are those who never try.

Ilka Chase

A model
for implementing this program

*Success in life is a matter
not so much of talent or opportunity
as of concentration and perseverance.*
—C.W. Wendte

*In this chapter I will show you how to make the most of this program. You may be feeling a bit overwhelmed at the moment. This chapter will erase the overwhelm and show you how to slowly implement the three steps in the **YASTYT** Program.*

Just for a moment I would like you to think back on the story of the farmer and his sheep. If you will recall, there were three parts to the story. The first illustration represented *Reception*. Remember? The farmer was opening the gate. The second illustration represented *Reorganization*. The farmer was cutting the sheep he wanted to keep. In the last illustration, the farmer was herding his sheep directly to the barn, which represented *Retention*.

Each step was important and contributed to the final outcome. Opening the gate is just as important to cutting the sheep as cutting the sheep is to getting them to the barn.

The **YASTYT** learning system functions in a similar way. All three parts are important and the Blending of these parts contributes to the end result. It is a simple system, and if you want to experience the full benefits, you must use all three parts: *Reception*, *Reorganization* and *Retention*.

By now, you have read the bulk of this book and have a fair grasp of the **YASTYT** learning system. You may feel a little apprehensive about trying these techniques on your next test because so much is at stake; therefore, I recommend the *Ease-In* method.

THE EASE-IN METHOD
First, don't try to go back and relearn everything you have had up to now using this system. For most of you that would be physically impossible. Start today and do what you can.

For a few days, commit yourself completely to using your *Reception* attribute only. No matter what you are doing make sure that the gate to your brain is open. Remember our farmer. Discover the most efficient ways to use this skill. Notice how much more you are receiving and remembering.

Remember that if you are an *Auditory Language Processor*, it would be in your best interest to find a *Combination Language Processor* you can work with. Smart students love to work with other students because statistically it increases the chance for success. Loners seldom do as well. Ed Halberg, Ph.D. and Kayleen Halberg, M.A., creators of *The College Success Factor Index*, have found that involvement with other students and faculty greatly enhances a student's chance for academic success.

Don't expect huge changes with the implementation of just your *Reception* attribute. Remember, this is a three-step process.

Once you feel comfortable using your *Reception* attribute, gradually begin to add the next step. Begin to *Reorganize* your reading material. Experiment with how to do this. Find the fastest, easiest way. Use your own ingenuity to modify the techniques given. Talk to other students and find out what they are doing. As you discover your system, notice how much more you are remembering.

When the *Reorganization* step feels comfortable, then add the *Retention* step. If you are an *Experiential Learner*, don't try to be a loner. Team up with other people. Remember, two heads are better than one. For those who are talented in *Knowing Self*, put a study group together and lead it. For those talented in *Knowing Others*, team up with people to help create *Experiential* learning situations and go to the learning lab.

Implement this one step at a time and I guarantee you will be thrilled with the results.

With this system my grades have gone from C's to A's, and I must say I don't blank out on tests any more.

-Washington
Spanish Major

Chapter 7

Confronting
test anxiety—head-on!

*If we have not peace within ourselves,
it is in vain to seek it from outward sources.*

—Rochefoucauld

In this chapter we look at two test strategies. 1) You will discover things you can do during tests that will stimulate the best parts of your brain and thus help you to function at a higher level. 2) You will also learn a technique that will completely alleviate test anxiety, if you will use it.

If you will look in *Appendix C*, you will find the *Application Chart*. Look down the left column for your attributes, then look across to the right of the column labeled *Testing*. You will find some helpful hints to use while taking a test.

There is one other thing that perhaps stands between you and success, and for some it is the ultimate equalizer. Here you are a diligent student. You have studied. You know the material— cold. But what looms ahead of you? THE TEST! And this scares you more than death itself.

I know. I have seen it. The bravest young men in my classes have been brought to their knees by a measly old test. How could that be? How could tests hold such power? They do. I say to you that today is a new day! I have a radical idea to pass on to you. What would happen to your life if you loved, I repeat, loved taking tests?

I want you to think about this for a minute. Would it change things? How?

I have asked my students this question and the first response is always a cynical one. "That is impossible." "I wouldn't want to." "To love an enemy, that would be unthinkable." Then, as the shock wears off, the light begins to come on.

"If I loved taking tests?" "I would study more." "I would have more fun studying." "I wouldn't dread homework as much." "I would like school more." "I would probably do much better on tests." "I would be an A student without the stress."

Yes, it is true. The unbelievable would be possible if you loved taking tests. It is the frosting on the cake to this system. Don't

With this system, I am spending less hours studying, and I find that I don't draw as many blanks as I used to.

-Pennsylvania
Nursing Student

This program helped me to look at studying and test taking in a better, more effective way.

-New York
Nursing Student

An entire class made t-shirts and posters to celebrate their final in a nursing class.

Some schools really get into the idea about saying "I love Taking Tests".

you think it is time to slay the dragon? How? It's easy.

Say to yourself:

I love taking tests!

Say it again and again and again for the next 21 days. The more times you say it, the better, and don't miss a day. You will begin to believe this phrase in a few days and you will be amazed at what begins to happen for you.

Every semester students have tried this, and the results have always been the same. They find themselves much calmer in a testing situation. They don't stress out like they have in the past. They make fewer "stupid" mistakes. They have fun and find that their grades just keep getting better. Students begin to love what they are doing. They begin to believe in themselves. You can, too.

When you say this phrase, say it aloud. Say it silently. Say it looking in the mirror. Say it on the way to class. Say it during tests. Say it when you get nervous. Say it before you go to sleep. Live with this phrase for the next 21 days. You will notice its effect.

You may be thinking, how can that be? Well, your mind is more powerful than your body. A number of years ago a study was done to test the power of the mind. Two basketball teams were assembled with the idea that in a few months they would play a game. The teams were equally matched with player size and ability. Then, the two teams were sent off to practice.

One team practiced in the traditional way. They worked out in the gym, shooting baskets, and running drills. The other team did something very different. All during the months of practice they never touched a basketball. They went to the gym, but instead of shooting baskets, they sat down and visualized the most perfect game. They visualized themselves in every possible situation. They saw themselves shooting perfect baskets, then aptly defending and blocking shots.

When the practice months were over, the two teams met to play a game to see who was the best team. The team that used their minds instead of their bodies to practice won the game hands down. The score was very lopsided in favor of the visualizers.

The point of this story is this: you will never enjoy taking tests until you have convinced your mind that you love taking tests. So, get started. It's icing on the cake.

Chapter 8

Conclusion
Making a difference!

Half the misery in the world comes of want of courage to speak, and to hear the truth plainly, and in the spirit of love.
—Harriet Beecher Stowe

This is not an ending, it is a beginning. A beginning to enjoy, appreciate, and win with who you are. Over the last few days you have taken a journey of discovery. This journey allowed you to uncover not only your personal attributes, but also how you can use these attributes to transform any learning situation into a winning situation.

As you learn to honor your unique qualities, these qualities will honor you and others. As you continue on this journey, you may discover that what was once an irritation will become a place of understanding and peace. We are all different and important. Your attributes are just as important as your neighbor's. Studies show that a classroom of diverse learners—students with a variety of learning attributes—learn better and faster than a group with like attributes. I am convinced that we are all different for a reason. As we offer our gifts to the world, and connect with others who do the same, wonderful things begin to happen. Together we complete the circle.

The following story was first published in the book, *Chicken Soup For the Soul*, by Jack Canfield and Mark Victor Hansen. It is titled, *Who You Are Makes a Difference*, and was written by Helice Bridges.

A teacher in New York decided to honor her high school seniors by telling them the difference they each made. Using a process developed by Helice Bridges of Del Mar, California, she called each student to the front of the class, one at a time. First she told them how the student made a difference to her and the class. Then she presented each of them with a blue ribbon imprinted with gold letters, which read, *Who I Am Makes a Difference.* Afterward the teacher decided to do

Life is a journey, not a destination.
Please remember this:

> Shoot for the moon. Even if you miss it, you will land among the stars.
> —*Les Brown*

My hope is that the story in this chapter will warm your heart, touch your soul, and send you on your way, whistling.

You give but little when you give of your possessions. It is when you give of yourself that you truly give.

Kahlil Gibran

a class project to see what kind of impact recognition would have on a community. She gave each of the students three more ribbons and instructed them to go out and spread this acknowledgment ceremony. Then they were to follow up on the results, see who honored whom, and report back to the class in about a week.

One of the boys in the class went to a junior executive in a nearby company and honored him for helping him with his career planning. He gave the executive a blue ribbon and put it on his shirt. Then, he gave him two extra ribbons and said, "We're doing a class project on recognition, and we'd like you to go out, find somebody to honor, give them a blue ribbon, then give them the extra blue ribbon so that they can acknowledge a third person and keep this acknowledgment ceremony going. Then please report back to me and tell me what happened."

Later that day the junior executive went in to see his boss, who had been noted, by the way, as being kind of a grouchy fellow. He sat his boss down and told him that he deeply admired him for being a creative genius. The boss seemed very surprised. The junior executive asked him if he would accept the gift of the blue ribbon and would give him permission to put it on him. His surprised boss said, "Well, sure."

The junior executive took the blue ribbon and placed it right on his boss's jacket above his heart. As he gave him the last extra ribbon, he said, "Would you do me a favor? Would you take this extra ribbon and pass it on by honoring somebody else? The young boy who first gave me the ribbon is doing a project in school and we want to keep this recognition ceremony going and to find out how it affects people."

That night the boss came home to his 14-year-old son and sat him down. He said, "The most incredible thing happened to me today. I was in my office and one of the junior executives came in and told me he admired me and gave me a blue ribbon for being a creative genius. Imagine. He thinks I'm a creative genius. Then he put this blue ribbon that says, *Who I Am Makes A Difference* on my jacket above my heart. He gave me an extra ribbon and asked me to find somebody else to honor. As I was driving home tonight, I started thinking about who I would honor with this ribbon and I thought about you. I want to honor you.

"My days are really hectic, and when I come home I don't pay a lot of attention to you. Sometimes I scream at you for not getting good enough grades in school and for your bedroom being a mess, but somehow tonight, I just wanted to sit here and, well, just let you know that you do make a difference to me. Besides your mother, you are the most important person in my life. You're a great kid and I love you!"

The startled boy started to sob and sob, and he couldn't stop crying. His whole body shook. He looked up at his father and said through his tears, "I was planning on committing suicide tomorrow, Dad, because I didn't think you loved me. Now I don't need to."

On the next page you will find a ribbon with the words, *Who You Are Makes a Difference*. I would like to present this ribbon to you. Please color it blue, cut it out, and pin it on yourself for me. Please do this. I want you to know that who you are is incredible and that your unique gifts touch each one of us.

On page 135 you will find six additional ribbons. I would like you to cut these out, also, and continue this acknowledgment ceremony. Acknowledge three more people and give each one of them an extra ribbon. Ask them to acknowledge someone else in their lives, and then ask them to report back to you. I would love to hear what happens.

We spend so much of our lives looking at how we fall short or how we don't measure up. I hope this book has opened your eyes to the idea that who you are is perfect. My wish for you is that you will continue to discover your gifts and share them with the world. Because after all, **You** *Are Smarter Than You Think!* and *Who You Are Makes a Difference*.

Alone we can do so little; together we can do so much.

-Helen Keller

"Who you are makes a difference," by Helice Bridges
Published in Chicken Soup for the Soul by Jack Canfield and Mark Victor Hansen, Copyright 1993.
Reprinted with permission from:
> *Health Communications, Inc.*
> *3201 S. W. 15th Street*
> *Deerfield Beach, FL 33442-8190*

This one is for YOU!

From the book:

YOU *ARE SMARTER*
THAN YOU THINK!

From the book:
YOU ARE SMARTER
THAN YOU THINK!

From the book:
YOU ARE SMARTER
THAN YOU THINK!

From the book:
YOU ARE SMARTER
THAN YOU THINK!

From the book:
YOU ARE SMARTER
THAN YOU THINK!

From the book:
YOU ARE SMARTER
THAN YOU THINK!

From the book:
YOU ARE SMARTER
THAN YOU THINK!

Appendix - A

A Note To The Instructor

Have you ever looked out over a sea of students whose lights were on but nobody was home? Or, have you been blamed by your students for their poor grades? If your answer is yes to either one of these questions, then you are sure to appreciate this book.

The **You** Are Smarter Than You Think! learning system is designed to empower your students. It teaches them how to transform any learning situation into a winning situation. When a student knows how they learn best, they become less dependent on the instructor, thus freeing you up to teach the way you were designed to teach. The classroom becomes a win/win situation. The instructor has more fun while the student is learning better than ever before.

Over the last thirteen years, I have discovered some things that might help with this book's implementation. First, even though this book can be read and applied without an instructor's help, any encouragement that you can give your students will increase their chances for success with the system. A simple aid you can offer is to write on the chalkboard before each test, **You** Are Smarter Than You Think! It is a simple thing to do and the students find it very helpful.

As your students begin to implement the **You** Are Smarter Than You Think! program, they will want to transform their learning environment into something that works for them. They need your support in this endeavor. Some of your students may ask if they can use a tape recorder in your class. If you can be comfortable with this, it will greatly enhance their success. Other students will just listen in class and will not take notes. Some will be using lots of colored pens to take their notes and some may even move their legs around a bit. They have been instructed not to disrupt the class with any of their actions. As you read through the book, you will begin to understand why the students are doing what they are doing. I thank you in advance for your willingness to accommodate these activities.

Another way you can assist your students is by paying attention to their *Reception* score. This score reflects their ability to process and remember language.

I have found that if you have a student whose scores in all three areas are five and below, this student may need some help with language processing. I recommend that you contact your English As A Second Language (ESL) program to tell them about my recommendation. Show them the activities in this book and I think they will know what to do. I have found over the years that students who score low in this area tend to

To love what you do, and feel that it matters—how could anything be more fun?

Katherine Graham

Imparting knowledge is only lighting other men's candles at our lamp, without depriving ourselves of any flame.

Jane Porter

As a nursing instructor, one of the most frustrating things I have had to deal with is the students who excel in working with patients and yet fail in the classroom. So often these students flunk out of the program due to low test scores and yet, in my heart, I know that if they could pass the tests they would make excellent nurses.

I have found a solution to this problem. The **YOU** ARE SMARTER THAN YOU THINK! *Learning System reaches these students. They suddenly discover how to learn. Almost overnight they become classroom successes.*

It makes me feel good to see these wonderful students succeed.

> Nancy English,
> Ph.D., R.N.
> Professor of Nursing
> Golden West College

I touch the future. I teach.

> Christa McAuliffe Educator

find nursing school, graduate programs, and law school very difficult. This is not a hopeless situation, however. I have had students with very low scores who were flunking nursing, and after one semester in ESL, rose to the top of their class.

Your students may resist the idea of going into ESL, but perhaps you and the ESL instructor together may be able to convince them of its importance. Many times, it is the bilingual students who have this difficulty. They speak well, but when it comes to reading and comprehending more difficult material, their encoding skills break down. These students may have already been through the ESL program. Insist that they return, because the level of language processing is much higher for some types of learning. Also, these students will struggle unnecessarily until this problem is corrected.

Another important concept that I have learned is that it frequently scares students to do things differently, especially something as basic as studying. Students need you to understand this. Providing an opportunity for them to express their concerns might also be helpful. I have found that simply through the expression of these feelings, the fears dissipate and the student can move on.

Finally, the following is a list of support materials that supplement this book:

- How to Have More Fun in the Classroom is a one-hour presentation designed to do just that—show you how to have more fun!

- The *You Are Smarter Than You Think!* Workshop is the practical application of the material in this book. It is a fun workshop and goes hand-in-hand with How to Have Fun in the Classroom.

- A 50-minute video introduces the *You Are Smarter Than You Think!* concept to students and fellow instructors.

- An audio version of the entire *You Are Smarter Than You Think!* book.

- If you would like further information contact:
  Renée Mollan-Masters, M.A.
  c/o Reality Productions
  6245 Old Hwy. 99 South
  Ashland, Oregon 97520
  Phone 541-482-3506
  www.youaresmarterthanyouthink.com

One final thought—*Thank you for all that you do!*

You Are Smarter Thank You Think!
Applicaton Chart

YOUR STYLE	Lecture	Textbook	Test Study	Test Taking
AUDITORY, LINGUISTIC, MUSICAL, BODY KINESTHETIC	Tape and listen to the lecture or listen and get notes from someone else. Move your body.	Hook up with a Combination Learner. Listen to the book as they read aloud. Organize the material using the modified highlighting technique.	Put what you want to learn on tape with background music playing. As you listen to the tape, move to the rhythm of the music.	Read carefully. Put your finger under each word and hear the word in your head. Talk to yourself about what is being asked.
AUDITORY, LINGUISTIC, MUSICAL, SELF KNOWING	Tape and listen to the lecture or listen and get notes from someone else.	Hook up with a Combination Learner. Listen to the book as they read aloud. Organize the material using the modified highlighting technique.	Put what you want to learn on tape. Do it as though you are teaching the information to someone. Have background music playing. Listen to the tape.	Read carefully. Hear the words in your head. Talk to yourself about what is being asked. Hear music in your head to relax.
AUDITORY, LINGUISTIC, MUSICAL, KNOWING OTHERS	Tape and listen to the lecture or listen and get notes from someone else.	Hook up with a Combination Learner. Listen to the book as they read aloud. Organize the material using the modified highlighting technique.	Put what you want to learn on tape, making sure to experientialize all material. Play background music while you are doing this. Listen to the tape.	Read carefully. Hear the words in your head. Talk to yourself about what is being asked. Hear music in your head to relax.
AUDITORY, LINGUISTIC, BODY KINESTHETIC, KNOWING SELF	Tape and listen to the lecture or listen and get notes from someone else. Move your body,	Hook up with a Combination Learner. Listen to the book as they read aloud. Organize the material, using the modified highlighting technique.	Put what you want to learn on tape. Do it as though you are teaching the information to someone. Listen to the tape while you move.	Read carefully. Follow each word with your finger and hear the words in your head. Talk to yourself about what you are being asked. Move.
AUDITORY, LINGUISTIC, BODY KINESTHETIC, KNOWING OTHERS	Tape and listen to the lecture or listen and get notes from someone else. Move your body.	Hook up with a Combination Learner. Listen to the book as they read aloud. Organize important information using the modified highlighting technique.	Put what you want to learn on tape. Make sure to experientialize all material. Move as you listen to the tape.	Read carefully. Hear the words in your head. Follow each word with your finger. Talk to yourself about what you are being asked. Move.

You Are Smarter Thank You Think!
Applicaton Chart

YOUR STYLE	Lecture	Textbook	Test Study	Test Taking
AUDITORY, LINGUISTIC, KNOWING SELF, KNOWING OTHERS	Tape and listen to the lecture or listen and get notes from someone else.	Hook up with a Combination Learner. Listen to the book as they read aloud. Organize important information using the modified highlighting technique.	Put what you want to learn on tape. Pretend that you are teaching someone who knows less than you. Experientialize difficult material. Listen to the tape.	Read carefully. Hear the words in your head. Follow each word with your finger as you read. Talk to yourself about what you are being asked.
AUDITORY, LOGICAL, MUSICAL, BODY KINESTHETIC	Tape and listen to the lecture or listen and get notes from someone else. Move.	Hook up with a Combination Learner. Listen to the book as they read aloud. Organize important information logically into categories. Move.	Organize all that you want to learn in a logical fashion. Put this on tape with background music playing. Move while you listen to the tape.	Read carefully. Hear the words in your head. Follow the words with your fingers. If confused, look at the question logically.
AUDITORY, LOGICAL, MUSICAL, KNOWING SELF	Tape and listen to the lecture or listen and get notes from someone else.	Hook up with a Combination Learner. Listen to the book as they read aloud. Organize important information logically into categories. Listen to background music.	Organize all that you want to learn in a logical fashion. Pretend that you are teaching the information to someone who knows less than you. Put this on tape with background music playing.	Read carefully. Hear the words in your head. If confused look at the question logically.
AUDITORY, LOGICAL, MUSICAL, KNOWING OTHERS	Tape and listen to the lecture or listen and get notes from someone else.	Hook up with a Combination Learner. Listen to the book as they read aloud. Organize important information logically into categories. Have instrumental music playing.	Organize all that you want to learn in a logical fashion. Experientalize difficult material. Have background music playing. Put this on tape. Listen to the tape.	Read carefully. Hear the words in your head to a rhythm. If confused look at the question logically.
AUDITORY, LOGICAL, BODY KINESTHETIC, KNOWING SELF	Tape and listen to the lecture or listen and get notes from someone else. Move.	Hook up with a Combination Learner. Listen to the book as they read aloud. Organize important information logically into categories. Move.	Organize all that you want to learn in a logical fashion. Put this on tape pretending that you are teaching someone who knows less than you. Move around as you listen to the tape.	Read carefully. Hear the words in your head. Follow the words with your finger. If confused look at the question logically.

You Are Smarter Thank You Think!
Applicaton Chart

YOUR STYLE	Lecture	Textbook	Test Study	Test Taking
AUDITORY, LOGICAL, BODY KINESTHETIC, KNOWING OTHERS	Tape and listen to the lecture or listen and get notes from someone else. Move.	Hook up with a Combination Learner. Listen to the book as they read aloud. Organize important information logically into categories. Move.	Organize all that you want to learn in a logical fashion. Put this on tape making sure to experientialize difficult material. Move around as you listen to the tape.	Read carefully. Hear the words in your head. Follow the words with your fingers. If confused, look at the question logically.
AUDITORY, LOGICAL, KNOWING SELF, KNOWING OTHERS	Tape and listen to the lecture or listen and get notes from someone else.	Hook up with a Combination Learner. Listen to the book as they read aloud. Organize important information logically into categories.	Organize all that you want to learn in a logical fashion. Put this on tape pretending that you are teaching someone who knows less than you. Experientialize difficult information. Listen to the tape.	Read carefully. Hear the words in your head. If confused, look at the question logically.
AUDITORY, SPATIAL, BODY KINESTHETIC, MUSICAL	Tape and listen to the lecture or listen and get notes from someone else. Move.	Hook up with a Combination Learner. Listen to the book as they read aloud. Organize the material into maps. Remember to move occasionally and have background music playing.	Organize all that you want to learn into categories and make sure everything is mapped. Put this on tape with background music. Listen to the tape and move to the rhythm of the music.	Read carefully. Hear what you are reading in your head. Look for the essence of the question. Move.
AUDITORY, SPATIAL, BODY KINESTHETIC, KNOWING SELF	Tape and listen to the lecture or listen and get notes from someone else. Move.	Hook up with a Combination Learner. Listen to the book as they read aloud. Organize the material into maps. Move.	Organize all that you want to learn in a logical fashion. Put this on tape pretending that you are teaching someone who knows less than you. Listen to the tape while you move.	Read carefully. Hear what you are reading in your head. Look for the essence of the question. Move.
AUDITORY, SPATIAL, BODY KINESTHETIC, KNOWING OTHERS	Tape and listen to the lecture or listen and get notes from someone else. Move.	Hook up with a Combination Learner. Listen to the book as they read aloud. Organize the material into maps. Move.	Organize all that you want to learn into categories and make sure everything is mapped. Put this on tape making sure to experientialize difficult information. Listen to the tape as you move around.	Read carefully. Hear what you are reading in your head. Look for the essence of the question. Move.

You Are Smarter Thank You Think!
Applicaton Chart

YOUR STYLE	Lecture	Textbook	Test Study	Test Taking
AUDITORY, SPACIAL, MUSICAL, KNOWING SELF	Tape and listen to the lecture or listen and get notes from someone else.	Hook up with a Combination Learner. Listen to the book as they read aloud. Organize the material into maps. Play background music.	Organize all that you want to learn into categories and make sure everything is mapped. Put this on tape, pretending you are teaching the material to someone who knows less. Also play background music. Listen to the tape.	Read carefully. Hear what you are reading in your head. Look for the essence of the question.
AUDITORY, SPACIAL, MUSICAL, KNOWING OTHERS	Tape and listen to the lecture or listen and get notes from someone else.	Hook up with a Combination Learner. Listen to the book as they read aloud. Organize the material into maps. Play background music.	Organize all that you want to learn into categories and make sure everything is mapped. Put this on tape experientializing difficult material. Also play background music. Listen to the tape.	Read carefully. Hear what you are reading in your head. Look for the essence of the question.
AUDITORY, SPACIAL, KNOWING SELF, KNOWING OTHERS	Tape and listen to the lecture or listen and get notes from someone else.	Hook up with a Combination Learner. Listen to the book as they read aloud. Organize the material into maps.	Organize all that you want to learn into categories and make sure everything is mapped. Put this on tape, pretending you are teaching the material to someone who knows less. Be sure to use experientializations.	Read carefully. Hear what you are reading in your head. Look for the essence of the question.
VISUAL, LINGUISTIC, MUSICAL, BODY KINESTHETIC	Key in on anything that is visual. Write down key words. Get notes from someone else. Move.	Read and organize important information, using the modified highlighting technique.	Read over your extracted notes, have instrumental music playing, and move to the rhythm.	Follow the words you are reading with your fingers. Move. Hear music in your head to relax yourself.
VISUAL, LINGUISTIC, BODY KINESTHETIC, KNOWING SELF	Key in on anything that is visual. Write down key words. Get notes from someone else. Move.	Read and organize important information, using the modified highlighting technique. Move occasionally.	Read over your extracted notes, pretend you are teaching someone who knows less than you as you do this. Move.	Follow the words you are reading with your fingers. Move.

You Are Smarter Thank You Think!
Applicaton Chart

YOUR STYLE	Lecture	Textbook	Test Study	Test Taking
VISUAL, LINGUISTIC, BODY KINESTHETIC, KNOWING OTHERS	Key in on anything that is visual. Write down key words. Get notes from someone else. Move.	Read and organize important information, using the modified highlighting technique.	Read over your extracted notes, experientialize the important material. Move.	Follow the words you are reading with your fingers. Move.
VISUAL, LINGUISTIC, MUSICAL, KNOWING SELF	Key in on anything that is visual. Write down key words. Get notes from someone else.	Read and organize important information, using the modified highlighting technique.	Read over your extracted notes, pretend you are teaching someone who knows less than you as you do this. Play background music.	Hear music in your head to lower your stress.
VISUAL, LINGUISTIC, MUSICAL, KNOWING OTHERS	Key in on anything that is visual. Write down key words. Get notes from someone else.	Read and organize important information, using the modified highlighting technique. Have background music playing.	Read over your extracted notes, experientialize the difficult material. Play background music.	Hear music in your head to lower your stress.
VISUAL, LINGUISTIC, KNOWING SELF, KNOWING OTHERS	Write down key words. Get notes from someone else. Key in on anything that is visual.	Read and organize important information, using the modified highlighting technique.	Read over your extracted notes, pretending you are teaching the material to someone who knows less. Experientialize difficult material.	If you get stuck pretend you are teaching the information to someone.
VISUAL, LOGICAL, BODY KINESTHETIC, MUSICAL	Write down key words. Get notes from someone else. Key in on anything that is visual.	Organize important information under major categories in a sequential logical format. Some will like outlines, others another format. Play background music and move often.	Organize the information you want to learn sequentially and logically under major categories. Read this material while you listen and move to instrumental music.	As you read follow the words with your finger. Hearing music in your head will relax you.

You Are Smarter Thank You Think!
Applicaton Chart

YOUR STYLE	Lecture	Textbook	Test Study	Test Taking
VISUAL, LOGICAL, BODY KINESTHETIC, KNOWING SELF	Write down key words. Get notes from someone else. Key in on anything that is visual.	Organize important information under major categories in a sequential logical format. Some will like outlines, others another format. Move.	Organize the information you want to learn sequentially and logically under major categories. Read the material pretending you are teaching it to someone who knows less. Move around.	As you read follow the words with your finger. If you get stuck, think like a teacher.
VISUAL, LOGICAL, BODY KINESTHETIC, KNOWING OTHERS	Write down key words. Get notes from someone else. Key in on anything that is visual.	Organize important information under major categories in a sequential logical format. Some will like outlines, others another format. Move.	Organize the information you want to learn sequentially and logically under major categories. Read the material, experientializing difficult material. Move often.	As you read follow the words with your finger.
VISUAL, LOGICAL, MUSICAL, KNOWING SELF	Write down key words. Get notes from someone else. Key in on anything that is visual.	Organize important information under major categories in a sequential logical format. Some will like outlines, others another format. Play background music.	Organize the information you want to learn sequentially and logically under major categories. Read the material pretending you are teaching it to someone who knows less. Have background instrumental music playing.	If you get stuck, pretend that you are the teacher.
VISUAL, LOGICAL, MUSICAL, KNOWING OTHERS	Write down key words. Get notes from someone else. Key in on anything that is visual. Hear background music in your head.	Organize important information under major categories in a sequential logical format. Some will like outlines, others another format. Play background music.	Organize the information you want to learn sequentially and logically under major categories. Read the material, experientializing difficult material. Play background music.	Hear background music in your head. It will relax you.
VISUAL, LOGICAL, KNOWING SELF, KNOWING OTHERS	Write down key words. Get notes from someone else. Key in on anything that is visual.	Organize important information under major categories in a sequential logical format. Some will like outlines, others another format.	Organize the information you want to learn sequentially and logically under major categories. Read the material pretending you are teaching it to someone who knows less. Make sure to experientialize difficult material.	If you get stuck, pretend that you are the teacher.

You Are Smarter Thank You Think!
Applicaton Chart

YOUR STYLE	Lecture	Textbook	Test Study	Test Taking
VISUAL, SPACIAL MUSICAL, BODY KINESTHETIC	Write down key words. Get notes from someone else. Key in on anything that is visual. Move.	As you read pull out important information an map it under major headings. Move. Have background music playing.	Review maps while moving to instrumental music.	Break down difficult questions into their essential parts. Move.
VISUAL, SPACIAL MUSICAL, KNOWING SELF	Write down key words. Get notes from someone else. Key in on anything that is visual.	As you read pull out important information and map it under major headings. Have background music playing.	Review maps while pretending to teach the material to someone who knows less than you Play background music.	Break down difficult questions into their essential parts and pretend that you are a teacher.
VISUAL, SPACIAL MUSICAL, KNOWING OTHERS	Write down key words. Get notes from someone else. Key in on anything that is visual.	As you read pull out important information and map it under major headings Have background music playing.	Review maps while experientializing difficult material.	Break down difficult questions into their essential parts.
VISUAL, SPACIAL BODY KINESTHETIC KNOWING SELF	Write down key words. Get notes from someone else. Key in on anything that is visual. Move.	As you read pull out important information and map it under major headings Move	Review maps while pretending to teach the material to someone who knows less than you Move around.	Break down difficult questions into their essential parts and pretend that you are a teacher.
VISUAL, SPACIAL BODY KINESTHETIC KNOWING OTHERS	Write down key words. Get notes from someone else. Key in on anything that is visual. Move.	As you read pull out important information and map it under major headings. Move.	Review maps while experientializing difficult material. Move around.	Break down difficult questions into their essential parts.

You Are Smarter Thank You Think!
Applicaton Chart

YOUR STYLE	Lecture	Textbook	Test Study	Test Taking
VISUAL, SPATIAL, KNOWING SELF, KNOWING OTHERS	Write down key words. Get notes from someone else. Key in on anything that is visual.	As you read pull out important information and map it under major headings.	Review maps while pretending you are teaching someone who knows less than you. Experientialize difficult material.	Break down difficult questions into their essential parts. If you really get stuck, pretend you are the teacher.
COMBINATION, LINGUISTIC, BODY KINESTHETIC, MUSICAL	Take notes. Use your own words to express what is said. Move.	Read aloud or subvocalize. Organize important information using the Modified Highlighting Technique. Have instrumental music playing. Move occasionally.	Read aloud your extracted notes. As you do this, listen to music and move to it.	Subvocalize what you read. Follow the words with your finger.
COMBINATION, LINGUISTIC, BODY KINESTHETIC, KNOWING SELF	Take notes. Use your own words to express what is said. Move.	Read aloud or subvocalize. Organize important information using the Modified Highlighting Technique. Pretend you are teaching the information to someone who knows less than you. Move.	Read aloud your extracted notes. Pretend you are teaching the information to someone. Move.	Subvocalize what you read. Follow the words with your finger.
COMBINATION, LINGUISTIC, BODY KINESTHETIC, KNOWING OTHERS	Take notes. Use your own words to express what is said. Move.	Read aloud or subvocalize. Organize important information using the Modified Highlighting Technique. Experientialize difficult material. Move.	Read aloud your extracted notes. Experientialize all difficult material. Move.	Subvocalize what you read. Follow the words with your finger.
COMBINATION, LINGUISTIC, MUSICAL, KNOWING SELF	Take notes. Use your own words to express what is said.	Organize important information using the Modified Highlighting Technique. Pretend you are teaching the information to someone who knows less than you. Play background music.	Read aloud your extracted notes. Pretend you are teaching the information to someone who knows less than you. Play background music.	Subvocalize what you read. Hear music in your head to relax yourself.

You Are Smarter Thank You Think!

Applicaton Chart

YOUR STYLE	Lecture	Textbook	Test Study	Test Taking
COMBINATION, LINGUESTIC, MUSICAL, KNOWING OTHERS	Take notes. Use your own words to express what is said.	Read aloud or subvocalize. Organize important information using the Modified Highlighting Technique. Experientialize difficult material. Play background music.	Read aloud your extracted notes. Experientialize all difficult material. Play background music.	Subvocalize what you read. Hear music in your head to relax yourself.
COMBINATION, LINGUESTIC, KNOWING SELF KNOWING OTHERS	Take notes. Use your own words to express what is said.	Read aloud or subvocalize. Organize important information using the Modified Highlighting Technique. Experientialize difficult material.	Read aloud your extracted notes, pretending you are teaching someone the information. Experientialize all difficult material.	Subvocalize what you read.
COMBINATION, LOGICAL, BODY KINESTHETIC, MUSICAL	Take notes. Organize the material in a logical sequential format.	Read aloud. Organize important information under major categories in a sequential logical format. Some will like outlines, other another format. Play background music and move.	Study aloud. Sing or read all your notes to music. Move to the music.	Subvocalize what you read. Follow the words with your finger.
COMBINATION, LOGICAL, MUSICAL, KNOWING SELF	Take notes. Organize the material in a logical sequential format. Move.	Read aloud. Organize important information under major categories in a sequential logical format. Some will like outlines, other another format. Move.	Read aloud your extracted notes. Pretend you are teaching the information to someone who knows less than you. Move around.	Subvocalize what you read. Move your finger under each word as you read it.
COMBINATION, LOGICAL, MUSICAL, KNOWING OTHERS	Take notes. Organize the material in a logical sequential format.	Read aloud. Organize important information under major categories in a sequential logical format. Experientialize abstract and difficult material. Move.	Study aloud. Organize all material into sequential logical format. Read all your notes aloud as you move around.	Subvocalize what you read. Move your finger under each word as you read it.

You Are Smarter Thank You Think!
Applicaton Chart

YOUR STYLE	Lecture	Textbook	Test Study	Test Taking
COMBINATION, LOGICAL, MUSICAL, KNOWING SELF	Take notes. Organize the material in a logical sequential format.	Read aloud. Organize important information under major categories in a sequential logical format. Some will like outlines, others another format. Play background music.	Read extracted notes aloud. Organize the material in a logical sequential format. Pretend you are teaching the information to some-one who knows less than you. Play music. You may want to sing what you are saying.	Subvocalize what you read. Hear music in your head to relax yourself
COMBINATION, LOGICAL, MUSICAL, KNOWING OTHERS	Take notes. Organize the material in a logical sequential format.	Read aloud. Organize important information under major categories in a sequential logical format. Some will like outlines, others another format. Play background music.	Read extracted notes aloud. Organize all material into sequential logical format. Experientialize difficult material. Play music. You may want to sing what you are saying.	Subvocalize what you read. Hear music in your head to relax yourself
COMBINATION, LOGICAL, KNOWING SELF KNOWING OTHERS	Take notes. Organize the material in a logical sequential format.	Read aloud. Organize important information under major categories in a sequential logical format. Some will like outlines, others another format.	Read extracted notes aloud. Organize all material into sequential logical format. Experientialize difficult material. Pretend you are teaching the information to some-one who knows less than you.	Subvocalize what you read.
COMBINATION, SPATIAL, BODY KINESTHETIC, MUSICAL	Take notes. Simplify what is said. Move.	Read aloud or subvocalize. Organize the material into major categories and then simplify it into maps. Have background music playing. Move occasionally.	Read aloud your maps of the material you want to learn. Do this to music, singing and moving to the rhythm.	Subvocalize the questions out loud softly or in your head. Follow the words with your finger as you read. Simplify question if it is difficult.
COMBINATION, SPATIAL, BODY KINESTHETIC, KNOWING SELF	Take notes. Simplify what is said. Move.	Read aloud or subvocalize. Organize the material into major categories and then simplify it into maps. Move.	Read aloud your maps of the material you want to learn. Pretend you are teaching someone. Move.	Subvocalize the questions out loud softly or in your head. Follow the words with your finger as you read. Simplify question if it is difficult.

You Are Smarter Thank You Think!
Applicaton Chart

YOUR STYLE	Lecture	Textbook	Test Study	Test Taking
COMBINATION, SPATIAL, BODY KINESTHETIC, KNOWING OTHERS	Take notes. Simplify what is said. Move.	Read aloud or subvocalize. Organize the material into major categories and then simplify it into maps. Move.	Read aloud your maps of the material you want to learn. Experientialize any material you are having difficulties with. Move	Subvocalize the questions out loud softly or in your head. Follow the words with your finger as you read. Simplify question if it is difficult.
COMBINATION, SPATIAL, MUSICAL, KNOWING SELF	Take notes. Simplify what is said.	Read aloud or subvocalize. Organize the material into major categories and then simplify it into maps. Have background music playing.	Read aloud your maps of the material you want to learn. Sing this material, pretending that you are teaching someone who knows less than you.	Subvocalize the questions out loud softly or in your head. Simplify question if it is difficult. Hear music in your head to relax yourself.
COMBINATION, SPATIAL, MUSICAL, KNOWING OTHERS	Take notes. Simplify what is said.	Read aloud or subvocalize. Organize the material into major categories and then simplify it into maps. Have background music playing.	Read aloud your maps of the material you want to learn. Sing the information an experientialize difficult material.	Subvocalize the questions out loud softly or in your head. Simplify question if it is difficult. Hear music in your head to relax yourself.
COMBINATION, SPATIAL, KNOWING OTHERS, KNOWING SELF	Take notes. Simplify what is said.	Read aloud or subvocalize. Organize the material into major categories and then simplify it into maps.	Read aloud your maps of the material you want to learn. Pretend you are teaching the material to someone. Experientialize difficult material.	Subvocalize the questions out loud softly or in your head. Simplify question if it is difficult.

My Personal Learning Summary

Success Map *(Tear this page out.)*

Name _____   Date _____

RECEPTION	page 43	Score	
Auditory Language Processor		_____	_____
Visual Language Processor		_____	_____
Combination Language Processor		_____	_____

REORGANIZATION	page 57	Score	
Attribute A - Linguistic		_____	_____
Attribute B - Logical		_____	_____
Attribute C - Spatial		_____	_____

RETENTION	page 101	Score	
Attribute D - Musical		_____	_____
Attribute E - Body Kinesthetic		_____	_____
Attribute F - Knowing Self		_____	_____
Attribute G - Knowing Others		_____	_____

An extra copy of this form can be found in the Appendix.

Tear out along this perforated edge.

Index

About The Author

Renée Mollan-Masters has been interested in the learning process for much of her adult life. She earned her Master's Degree in Speech Pathology from California State University, Fullerton. While serving as Speech Pathologist for the Fountain Valley School District, she developed a reading perception lab that became a model program for the state of California. Later, Renée was in private practice in speech pathology for a number of years.

In 1980, Renée wrote *Yes They Can*, a handbook for effectively parenting the disabled. She also held workshops and lectured nationally on the subject.

Renée developed **You** *Are Smarter Than You Think!* in 1987, and taught it to college students all over Southern California. She later refined the program for Orange Coast College, where she included it in the *How To Survive College* class curriculum.

In 1992, the first edition of her book, **You** *Are Smarter Than You Think!* was published. This Learning System is used in colleges and universities throughout the country. Her hope is that this system will make education a more equitable and worthwhile experience for students everywhere.

Renée currently lives with her husband in the mountains just outside Ashland, Oregon.

You Are Smarter Than You Think!

Products and Services

Reality Productions is proud to present the following materials and services designed to support students and teachers in winning from the *You* Are Smarter Than You Think! (*YASTYT*) Learning System.

THE BOOK—*You* Are Smarter Than You Think! evaluates the reader's learning style and then shows how to specifically apply this information to succeed academically.

> **COST:** $24.95 + $6.00 shipping. Bookstore/volume discounts are available (see website).

THE WEBSITE—www.youaresmarterthanyouthink.com is the official website for this book. It contains loads of ideas and support information for students and teachers. Check it out.

THE VIDEO—Renée Mollan-Masters, M.A. explains the overall concept of the *You* Are Smarter Than You Think! Learning System in this 50-minute video. Many schools have found this to be an effective tool for introducing the *You* Are Smarter Than You Think! Learning System to their students and faculty. COST: $30.00 + $6.00 shipping.

THE AUDIO TAPE—This is the *You* Are Smarter Than You Think! book on tape. Schools have made this tape available to students in their learning labs. It assists nonreaders work through the *You* Are Smarter Than You Think! book.

> **COST:** Two-tape set $10.00 + $6.00 shipping. Pilot schools receive one free copy of these tapes.

THE WORKSHOP—This is the original five-hour workshop, which presents the *You* Are Smarter Than You Think! Learning System. It is a fun, hands-on experience. Teachers find it helpful in fully understanding the program. Most pilot schools begin their pilot experience with this workshop.

> **COST:** $75.00 per participant. Each participant receives a copy of the *You* Are Smarter Than You Think! book as a part of their fee. Minimum of 15 participants is required with a maximum of 50.

THE PRESENTATION—How To Have More Fun Teaching is an hour-long experience presented by Renée Mollan-Masters, M.A., which unravels the traditional role of learning styles and challenges instructors to honor their uniqueness. Instructors walk away feeling new hope and excitement for what they do. This is an excellent program for your professional growth days. Up to 50 participants.

> **COST:** $1000.00 for up to 500 participants, plus travel expenses.

For more information on any of the above products and services, please contact:

Reality Productions
6245 Old Hwy. 99 South
Ashland, Oregon 97520
Phone: (541) 482-3506
yastyt@mind.net

Notes

Notes

Notes

Notes

Notes

Notes

Notes

Notes